ALBERT W. KETÈLBEY 1875 - 1959

From the Sanctuary of his Heart

ALBERT W. KETÈLBEY
(1875 - 1959)

From the Sanctuary of his Heart

Reflections on the life
of the Birmingham born composer

With a concise biography of his brother,
the virtuoso violinist
HAROLD GEORGE KETÈLBEY
(1883 - 1965)

JOHN SANT

FOREWORD BY MAJOR PATRICK M.H. DUNN R.M.

ALBERT W. KETÈLBEY 1875 - 1959

From the Sanctuary of his Heart

Reflections on the life of the Birmingham born composer

With a concise biography of his brother the virtuoso violinist

HAROLD GEORGE KETÈLBEY (1883 - 1965)

John Sant

Published by Manifold Publishing,
Manifold Gardens, 22 Beacon View Drive,
Sutton Coldfield, West Midlands, B74 2AW.

ISBN 0 9538058 0 8

Printed and bound in Great Britain by
Antony Rowe Ltd., Chippenham, Wiltshire.

Cover design by Adventure Graphic Communications,
Sutton Coldfield, West Midlands.

A.W.K. working at his favourite Victorian writing desk. Circa 1955.

To my Roberta and to the memory of William J. Neve.

..............whatsoever things are true,
whatsoever things are honest, whatsoever
things are just, whatsoever things are
pure, whatsoever things are lovely,
whatsoever things are of good report.........
.........think on these things.

Philippians 4 v 8.

Contents

ACKNOWLEDGEMENTS

Barbara Neve: I have a deep sense of gratitude to Barbara for the files on her late husband's own research work into the life of Ketèlbey, which she so kindly and generously gave to me. This work was undertaken by William in the years 1974/5 and amongst much factual information, produced several letters from people who had known the composer, and without which this book would be very much the poorer.

William J. Neve. B.A., A.R.A.M. (1911 - 1989): Born and brought up in Bournemouth, where he was educated at Bournemouth School, and following which he attended the Royal Academy of Music where he studied piano and organ. He joined the R. A. F. where he worked in Photographic Intelligence, serving much of the war in India. In 1946 he was appointed Director of Music at Cheltenham Grammar School, which post he held for 25 years until 1971. On retirement he became involved in writing programme notes for concerts and music criticisms for the local Cheltenham newspaper, and after spending many months researching the life of Ketèlbey, although his idea of writing a biography was not realised, he did write several excellent articles on the composer, and notably those which appeared in *The Lady* August 1975 and *Cotswold Life* January 1976.

Tom McCanna: Tom who is Music Librarian at Sheffield University has been researching the music of Ketèlbey for over 25 years, and in 1998 produced an excellent catalogue covering all of the composer's works. Tom's knowledge of Ketèlbey's music surpasses all others, and his generosity of spirit in providing me with a vast amount of information on both musical and biographical aspects of the composer's life, has saved me months of additional research work. In further doing what has almost amounted to a copy editing job on my manuscript, and sending me 15 A4 pages containing over 60 points of thought for revision, he has made this book richer and left me with a heart full of gratitude to a very humble and kind man. I am convinced that with his musical expertise Tom would have been the better man to write a more exhaustive and comprehensive book than this.

Major Patrick M. H. (Paddy) Dunn R.M.: In discovering the close bond of friendship which existed between Albert W. Ketèlbey and Captain William J. Dunn and his son Sir Vivian Dunn, I just knew who I should ask to write the Foreword to this book. Paddy Dunn is the grandson and son respectively of the above, and I thank Paddy not only for agreeing to do this, but also for his encouragement and kindness in providing me with much information concerning Ketèlbey's association with his family.

John Ambler and Colin Dean: As fellow members of the International Military Music Society (John Ambler being Chairman and Colin Dean Vice Chairman of the United Kingdom [Founder Branch]) I thank John and Colin for a wealth of newspaper cuttings and other research information concerning Ketèlbey's association with the military. Their generosity and encouragement in this respect has been an excellent example of promoting research - being one of the fundamental aims of the Society they represent. They have certainly been living proof of this to me.

Jean Penketh: As Ketèlbey's great niece I am grateful to Jean for the sheer joy she has brought to my work, in being the great fun loving character that she is. I thank her particularly for the many leads she gave, so enabling me to draw up an accurate picture of the Ketelbey family in Birmingham.

I am also grateful to the following for providing information and help on many aspects in connection with my research work:- Dr. Carl Chinn, Howard Friend, Stanley Smith, Margaret Lewis, Cynthia Holden, Mark Aston, Richard Smout, Peter Gammond, John Gough, Brother Ninian Arbuckle ofm, Brother Joe O'Toole ofm, Harry Green, Marie Haddleton, John Watson, Christopher Richards, Lawrence Wrigley, Kenneth Hinton, Phylis Eastgate, John Ward, Norman Aplin, Phil Yeomans, Michael Potter, Pastor Henry Sant, the late Stuart Upton and the late Wilfred Dorrington. The City Archive, the Music Dept., the Local Studies Dept. and the Art Dept. of Birmingham Central Library, Worcester City Library, I.O.W. County Library, Trinity College of Music, Royal College of Music, Royal Military School of Music, The Royal Archives, The Elgar Birthplace Museum, British Broadcasting Corporation, HNH International Ltd., Select Music and Video Distribution Ltd., The Theatre Museum, Birmingham Probate Registry, Birmingham Oratory, St. John's Church - Wimbledon, The Triumphant Church of God - Lozells.

Last but not least I thank my wife Roberta for putting up with Albert for so long!
Not only for processing and formatting the various drafts of my manuscript, but also for her patience, full support, assistance and suggestions, and not least for accompanying me on every long distance journey I have had to make to various parts of the country, in connection with my research work. I am particularly grateful to her for the meticulous job of collating information and painstakingly putting together for me the family tree of the Ketelbey family.

FOREWORD

In a battered but much cherished scrapbook which my grandmother preserved to record the last years of Captain W. J. 'Paddy' Dunn MVO MC, Director of Music of the Royal Horse Guards (The Blues) 1927 - 35, I learned much as a child about the grandfather I never knew and, in particular, his love of good music. From its fading newsprint, mostly the carefully constructed prose of numerous music critics, I read about the rapturous applause which seemed to be synonymous with his concerts, especially when they featured works by the giants of the light orchestral and band repertoires: Coates, Delibes, Tchaikovsky, Elgar, Schubert, Glinka, Strauss and so on. But there was one name which recurred more frequently than any other, that of his friend, Albert Ketèlbey.

These cuttings also document a number of occasions when my father, Sir Vivian Dunn, at that time during the 1930s Director of Music of Portsmouth Division Royal Marines and of the Royal Yacht Victoria and Albert, had been invited to Brighton to guest conduct his father's equally famous orchestra. Similarly the Ketèlbey concert on 12th February 1938 performed by the City of Portsmouth orchestra at Kingsway hall in London when my father assisted the famous maestro in conducting a programme devoted entirely to the great man's compositions. How I wish a recording had been taken to capture for posterity what must have been one of the most moving and satisfying musical experiences of the pre-war period: the privilege of hearing the composer's own interpretation of his principal works.

Throughout the war years, when Vivian Dunn recorded literally dozens of ENSA programmes for broadcast world-wide by the Overseas Recorded Broadcast Service as part of the entertainment and morale raising effort for Allied servicemen serving around the globe and for civilians at home, Ketèlbey's compositions featured increasingly prominently. *Bells across the Meadows, Gallantry, Sanctuary of the Heart, In a Persian Market, Cockney Suite* and countless others continued to stand alongside the works of more modern composers such as Novello, Gershwin, Leroy Anderson, Berlin, Rodgers and Kern. Post war, during the Royal Tours to South Africa in 1947 and to the Commonwealth in 1953 - 54, again a Ketèlbey composition such as *Wedgwood Blue* and *A Dream of Christmas* was invariably included in the music programmes for formal and informal occasions when the Royal Family entertained heads of state and other distinguished guests. Thus in a Richard Baker interview for his BBC music programme 'Comparing Notes' in 1988, when asked if an indication of the Royal Family's tastes in music could be given, my father replied: "Well, could I just say that we used to plant a great many trees in the monastery garden!" This exquisite piece was a particular favourite of King George V and I doubt there could have been a finer tribute to the immense popularity of such a characteristic composition.

This long overdue book faithfully and sensitively captures the remarkable career of one of England's finest composers. I have no doubt at all that those who have the good fortune to read it will feel compelled to discover or re-explore the full range of his quite extraordinary musical talent, an innate but highly developed genius which to this day undoubtedly continues to enrich the lives of lovers of good music everywhere. As the eminent musician, Jack Brymer, succinctly observed: 'There is something that cannot be put into words in all great music and it has nothing whatever to do with the art of music; it has to do with love.'

Albert Ketèlbey was indeed a magnificent craftsman of British Light Music whose skill was justly and universally recognised. His music of love and romance is enduring and seems as close to us today as breath itself.

Paddy Dunn
London   April 2000

All that is worthy of attainment is born out of struggle.

Anon.

ℐn painting his sometimes romantic, sometimes pastoral, sometimes religious, sometimes oriental, sometimes mythical and sometimes amusing musical pictures - of the moonlight, the meadows, the monastery, the Chinese garden, the Nile, etc. - Albert W. Ketèlbey in his unique style , had a gift, a yearning, a desire - whatever you like to call it - to arouse in his listener something warm, something deeper, something of much more meaning than the picture itself. This seems to be the crux of it all and is perhaps the reason why so many took, and still take, his unique music to their hearts.

Could this be the reason why on one hand some 'expert' critics have in the past criticised his music for being over sentimental, showy, too broad and even gaudy; and yet on the other an expert of perhaps another kind wrote these words of his music in an article which appeared in the *Birmingham Despatch* on the 1st August 1928:-

> "Romance is the key by which Mr. Ketèlbey unlocked the magic gate leading to fame with the great British public! That subtle, almost indefinable, mystic something which softens hearts and lulls one almost into tears is the formula - very difficult to discover - of finding success with the many. It has been adopted by musicians, painters, novelists, actors, singers for centuries past. It may not be highly intellectual, but it is clean and honest and entertaining".

A man of predominant musical fame between the war years of the twentieth century, and as a composer noted for his brilliance in orchestration, Ketèlbey surely deserves a more prominent place amongst that band of composers who between 1880 and 1950 gave us our musical inheritance in what we now call British light music. Of this stature there should be no doubt, some even referring to him in the past as "King of Light Music", a title sometimes given to another 'giant' of British light music, namely Eric Coates (1886 - 1957). In fact in terms of earnings, Ketèlbey and Coates were the most popular British composers of their time, Ketèlbey actually becoming the first ever millionaire British composer. For the unique and significant contributions each were to make to British light music perhaps both deserve the title for each man's season of success, whereby in the 1920s I believe it was surely Ketèlbey's, whose own music and popularity was to be eclipsed by that of Coates in the 1930s. Equally, there is no doubt that there is some continuing criticism - and even ridiculing - of Ketèlbey's music. Whilst some of this is attributable to musical snobbery (with some critics today continuing to demean even the music of the Johann Strauss dynasty) some is I believe attributable to Ketèlbey himself, through his persistence in seeking recognition as a 'serious' music composer, and in so doing unknowingly belittling his own genius for light music composition.

Several writers have previously stated that Ketèlbey retired to live a quiet life on the Isle of Wight when in his forties; however, this is not completely true as we shall see. A Trojan worker, a self-confessed perfectionist and very meticulous in all that he did, he once said at the height of his success, "I never consider a composition finished until, to my mind, no single note of it can be altered without spoiling it. I have invariably found that a splendid test, but before it can be passed I frequently revise a piece time after time. It all means hard work, but the responsiveness of the public is very satisfying reward."

Some have said that he could on occasions be, or appear to be, pompous, whilst on the other hand some have referred to him as a self-effacing man. In essence he was a very private, quiet, kind and retiring gentleman who did not like fuss, traits which he would not surrender to the fame and fortune which his success was to bring him. His very private nature was perhaps epitomised by his abhorrent dislike of being criticised, a trait which could unleash a rather uncharacteristically fierce response to those "who were to tread on his feet", which as we shall see did little to help his cause.

Whilst the efforts of several journalists and other professional enquirers of his life were proven negative when they tried to obtain thoughts, experiences and memories from the man himself, on those rare occasions when he did "open up the shell" quite often this would be with some unknown mortals. With Wilfred Dorrington his regular taxi driver whilst living in retirement on the Isle of Wight, he was always willing to talk about himself and his musical career, as he was during a brief chance meeting with Kenneth Hinton, an electrical shop manager from Birmingham, when the latter was on holiday in 1947. So too with Stanley Smith a Birmingham musician and life long fan of Ketèlbey, the composer promptly replied to Stanley's letter when he wrote to him in the 1950s, even sending him the personalised autograph as shown on page 5.

Several years ago I read these words of Jack Brymer O.B.E., the celebrated and popular clarinettist, professor and musical writer:-

> "There is something that cannot be put into words in all great music, and it has nothing whatever to do with the art of music: it has to do with love".

I still find these words very moving and by my own experience very true, in enjoying a wide repertoire of serious classical music of the romantic era, Viennese music of the Johann Strauss era, all original military music and in more recent years what I see as happy and yet very meaningful music of the British light music era. In this musical adventure of recent years I have to admit that much of it has also been like a nostalgic adventure, when in immediately recognising many tunes (but not previously knowing their title) and realising that this was attributable to my mother and father's love of listening to the radio, before we had a television, when every Friday night the music of *Friday Night is Music Night* had come in to my young heart.

We seem to live now in a world which loves bad news and readily disregards and throws away things of value and virtue once cherished by Britons and admired by the rest of the world. In music, it often appears that popular hype rather than real talent too often dictates success. These are good enough reasons why in recent years my love for happy yet meaningful music, which probably expresses some of those talents, values and virtues of old has grown - and hence my perpetual love of Ketèlbey's music, which has ultimately led me to writing this book. The story goes that in the 1930s an enthusiastic admirer rushed up to him and said, "Oh Mr. Ketèlbey, I know all your six pieces". "Six!" came the reply, "More like six hundred". Whilst his reply may have been a little on the optimistic side, Ketèlbey did write close on 400 pieces of a mixed genre of music, which are all detailed in my friend Tom McCanna's excellent catalogue *The Music of Albert W. Ketèlbey**. In this book I do not refer to all of these, but only to those popular and perhaps less popular light compositions and those serious - mainly piano - compositions which have become the bench marks of his life.

His success in living a very private life coupled with the facts that most of his contemporaries are now gone, that archives have apparently been destroyed or lost, and that following his death, his wife would not release any of his private papers (through his own expressed wishes) are the reasons why so little is known of his private life and consequently why so little has

---

* Enquiries to the author at Sheffield University.

been written about him. In turn these are the reasons why this book can in no way be called a full biography. In his lifetime Albert W. Ketèlbey preferred to talk of and sing the praises of others rather than himself, and so in that respect he would I believe be pleased with that situation.

In writing about the music of Ketèlbey in the *Daily Telegraph* on 26th July 1954, the pianist and writer Martin Cooper said, "The historian who examines the repertory of popular music played in England during the first half of the present century will have to reckon with Ketèlbey". I have no problem with that challenge at all, as I am confident that what little I have been able to write about him in the following pages places him on high account in our country's musical history for this period. I just wish that those who currently hold office and civic responsibility in Birmingham, the city of his birth, would take heed of such words and give their musical son even the minutest of recognition, which their forebears have failed so pitifully and miserably to give him in the past.

In an article written by Arthur Steele which appeared in the *Birmingham Evening Mail* on 20th December 1975, the point was raised that Birmingham had failed to pay any tribute to its most successful musical son in the centenary year of his birth, thus leaving the composer as "Birmingham's forgotten genius of melody". This article was to be the catalyst to rouse much interest in the form of letters and telephone calls from all over the country, pouring into the offices of the *Evening Mail*, and which in turn led to another reporter, Fred Norris, writing other articles in the newspaper, after carrying out his own investigations. Alas, as interesting as all of this was, with many calling for some form of recognition by the city of his birth, it was all to no avail as far as the city paying any form of tribute then, or indeed in the quarter of a century since. This neglect has in turn been the catalyst to enthuse me with the determination to write and publish this book in time for and in tribute of the 125th anniversary of Ketèlbey's birth in the millennium year 2000 - and even if I should be as one crying in the wilderness - then so be it!

This then is simply a reflection of the music man's life by an ordinary 'Brummie' who appreciates and cherishes the music of a fellow 'Brummie', who rose from his family roots in the back houses of the back streets of mid-nineteenth century industrial Birmingham, to the pinnacle of musical success of his day, and if the eye of the reader can eventually lead to his/her ear listening to some of that music, then I will be pleased - and I have a shrewd suspicion that Albert would be too..........

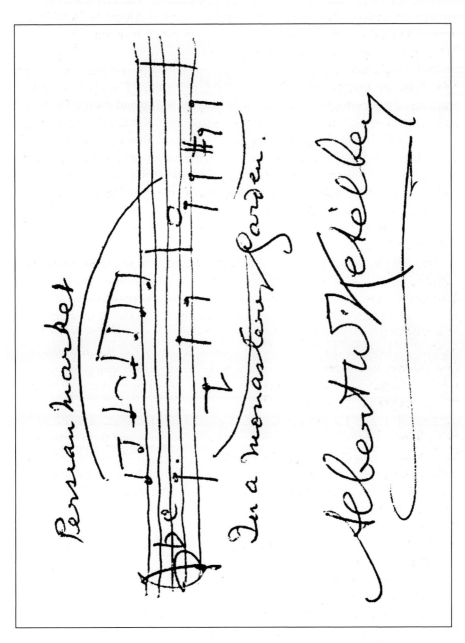

Personalised autograph sent to Stanley Smith.

CHAPTER 1

DISCOVERY AND ALMA STREET

Once I came upon a path I had not planned to take,
But curiosity came that day and won me for its sake,
And now I'm glad I've walked that path, with pastures
wide and new,
For by it's trail of providence it meant that I found you.

James Shakespeare.

S ome sceptics may ask the question, "What of any good ever came out of Aston?", to which the "Perry Barrionite" sceptic may answer "Birchfield Road", being the road which leads to Perry Barr! As a lad I would have answered the sceptics question with the words "Aston Villa", but now, although still a 'Villa Man' at heart, I would have to put before the famous football club the words Albert William Ketèlbey - Birmingham's own genius son of British light music.

In truth, of course, much besides of good and interest has come from this part of Birmingham. To name a few, a keen historian would refer us to Aston Hall built in 1635 and the home of the famous Holte family; the discerning ale drinker would refer us to Ansells old full bodied mild, brewed at Aston Cross; the epicurean would refer us to the world famous *H P Sauce* blended also at Aston Cross; and the industrial historian would refer us to the many companies which were born and grew on the demands for their skills in producing the "nuts and bolts" of British industry.

Having enjoyed listening to music from an early age, it was when I was a boy of about 12 years of age that I realised how much I appreciated good music, when for the first time, in a school music lesson, I heard Tchaikovsky's *1st Piano Concerto*, which simply enthralled me. From then on I just wanted to listen to and discover more of this kind of music. From the time I started earning money in my apprenticeship years I loved (and still do) visiting the famous record stores and searching through myriad

L.P.s to find that music which I knew would continue to enthral me. It was during such a hunt on one Saturday in the early 1970s that perchance I came upon an L.P. called *The World of Albert Ketèlbey* which had been issued by the Decca Record Company in 1971.

I had never heard of this Albert Ketèlbey before, but I remember holding that L.P. sleeve in my hand and reading the musical titles it contained - *In a Monastery Garden*, *Bells across the Meadows*, *Sanctuary of the Heart*, etc., and I just knew I had got to buy it. And so that Saturday night I had my first real taste of Albert William Ketèlbey, and that same night played his music over and over again, and had become 'hooked' on this sometimes amusing, sometimes moving, and nearly always picturesque music.

It was in January 1976 through Fred Norris's article in the *Birmingham Evening Mail* that I discovered that Ketèlbey was born in Alma Street, Birmingham - the same street in which my late mother whose name was Elma was born, and just around the corner from 11 Gerrard Street, where I was born 73 years after the birth of Albert. This fact intensified my interest in his music and also in the man, and led me to collect over the years any cuttings or snippets of information I could obtain about this quiet and reserved man who I believed through his musical genius had unknowingly bared the "Sanctuary of His Heart"!

I remember vividly the Victorian houses - two rooms up and two down - with their large round door handles on the front doors which from the polished cardinal red doorsteps led straight onto Alma Street. I remember too the long dark, spooky entry built in typical Victorian style from dark blue engineering bricks, which led to 1 back of 67 Alma Street where my 'Little Nan' (Dad's mother) lived, and also the not so long entry on the other side of the road which led to 1 back of 32 Alma Street, where my 'Big Nan' (Mom's mother) lived and where indeed my mother was born.

Next to 'Big Nan's' entry was the Salutation Inn public house and at the top of the street by the junction of 'Six Ways' was the local post office - opposite another public house called the Royal Exchange (see plate 12). Scattered throughout the street were several of what we 'kids' called 'sweet-shops', which were in fact small general stores sometimes occupying just the front room of the house, and from which you could buy a wide selection of goods. If one did not have what you were after, the chances were that another one would!

It was into this part of Birmingham - then called Aston Manor[1], Warwickshire, but without the Guy buses and Standard Vanguards and Morris Minors of the 1950s, that Albert William Ketelbey was born at 41 Alma Street, on 9th August 1875 to George Henry a jewellery engraver and his wife Sarah Ann née Aston, and brother to 20 months old Florence Beatrice.

1 Aston Manor, which was recorded in the Domesday Book as Estone, was incorporated within Birmingham on the 9th November 1911, when it became known as Aston.

George Henry Ketelbey was born on 2nd August 1854 at 16 Court, St. Georges Street, Hockley, Birmingham; brother to Eunice and son by the second marriage of Frederick William Ketelbey, a jeweller, and later a precision chaser, to Caroline nèe Smith-Phillips, who was the daughter of a certain Thomas Phillips, a japanner. Sarah Ann Aston was born on 15th January 1855 at Back of 87 Tennant Street, Edgbaston, Birmingham, daughter to Joseph Aston, a french plater, and later a gun stocker and then bankruptcy clerk of the Civil Court, and his wife Jemima nèe Whitehouse. Albert's grandfather Frederick William Ketelbey had had another seven children (two who died in infancy) by his first marriage to the late Charlotte nèe Hart.

George Henry and Sarah Ann had been married on 21st April 1873 at St. Matthias' Church (consecrated 1856 and closed 1949) on the corner of Wheeler Street and Farm Street, Hockley (see plate 5), and following their marriage went to live at 7 Richmond Terrace, Bridge Street West, Hockley where Florence was born on 11th December 1873. The family had moved to 41 Alma Street sometime during 1875, and some interesting facts concerning Albert's birthplace were that the house was owned by a certain Joseph Twist, to whom George Henry paid an annual rent of £10.00, and with a rateable value of £8.00 and an annual rate of 6d (2.5 pence) in the pound, "For the poor of the area" paid an annual rate of 4/- (20 pence)!

In 1875 the predominant form of transport was still the horse, with horse drawn trams and buses and the Hansom cab still very much in use by the gentry. For ladies, modesty still dictated that skirts and dresses touched the floor, very often worn with a bustle, and the sight of men in shining top hats was as regular as the sight is today of young men wearing baseball caps! With the splendid Council House in Colmore Row still in the process of being built, the Mayor of Birmingham at the time was the famous Joseph Chamberlain, who did much to improve the welfare of the residents of the city, and who was the father of Neville Chamberlain, Lord Mayor from 1915 to 1917 and Prime Minister from 1937 to 1939. From *Kelly's Directory of Birmingham* for 1875 it can be seen that Alma Street was an "Aladdin's Cave" of small businesses, and even at 39 next to the Ketelbeys there was a certain Miss Mary Hannah Allen - a shopkeeper.

Alas, this part of Birmingham is no longer as it was in the days of Ketelbey or indeed the earlier days of the writer, as in the interests of so-called progress all the houses in Alma Street north of Gerrard Street junction, and that part of Gerrard Street which ran to the junction of Wheeler Street, were demolished in the 1960s, to make way for high-rise flats, maisonettes, factories, a school and the Newtown Shopping Centre, in one of the city's

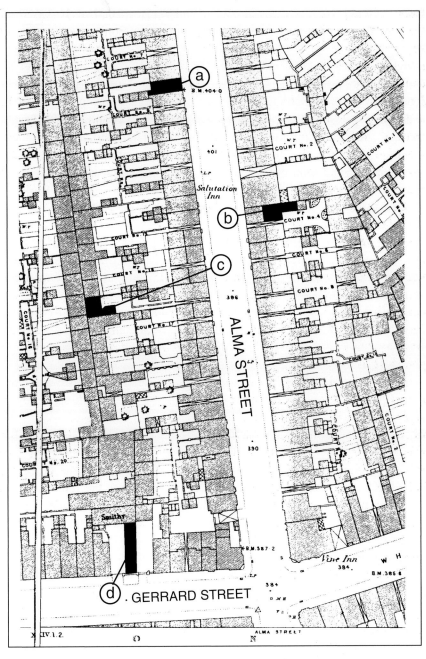

1888 map of part of old Alma Street showing (a) Ketèlbey's birthplace, (b) and (c) the homes of the author's grandparents and (d) the author's birthplace.

disastrous improvement programmes. The demise of the Aston area from that of being predominantly residential over a hundred years ago, to that of being predominantly industrial incorporating major infrastructural roads, and nowadays defined as "inner-city", can be seen in estimated population figures - in 1888 the population was approximately 66,000, whereas in 1979 it was less than 13,000.

During a pilgrimage to my birthplace on one sunny morning in March 1998, by using an old A to Z map and cross-referring it to a new one and with my memory of the area I was able to discover that the area which formed this part of Alma Street is now a play area, and what was once that old part of Gerrard Street where I was born is now Rodway Close. With my memory, some further patience, and perhaps even some fortitude, I was able to pace out and measure the approximate spot where Ketelbey's birthplace would have been (see plate 13).

With my to-ing and fro-ing and pacing and photographing, those residents who looked down on me from the surrounding high-rise flats, must have wondered what the dickens I was up to!

CHAPTER 2

ROOTS

By wisdom a house is built, and through understanding it is established; through knowledge its rooms are filled with rare and beautiful treasures.

Solomon.

The name Ketelbey is certainly a very unusual one, and is said to be Scandinavian - probably of Danish origin. Some earlier researchers and writers did not believe this to be the composer's real name but rather a pseudonym, quoting his real name as A. W. Aston, but as we shall see later, the opposite was in fact true. Indeed as recently as the early 1970s Aston was believed by many to be his real name, until in January 1976, Fred Norris of the *Birmingham Evening Mail* put this theory to flight, when during his own research work he un-earthed a copy of Albert William KETELBEY's original birth certificate. Remarkably there are still some writers who do not believe his name was Ketelbey, and even as recently as 1999 one individual when writing the programme note for one of Ketelbey's compositions performed at a light music concert in Sheffield, insisted that his real name was Aston! What probably added to the confusion of earlier researchers in this respect was the fact that at the time of Albert's birth there was indeed a George and Sarah Ann ASTON, who lived at 157 Wheeler Street on the borders of Aston Manor and Hockley, and who ironically also had a daughter named Florence who had been born, the day after Albert's own sister Florence, on 12th December 1873! Albert's real surname seems to have been spelt differently in different generations of the family, i.e. Kettelby, Kettelbey, Ketelby, etc. and on the birth certificate of father George Henry his surname is in fact spelt KETTLEBEY. At some time in his early life, however, his family changed the spelling to read KETELBEY, which is how it read on George Henry's marriage certificate. Even then the name was very often spelt incorrectly in documents, articles, directories, and even on such as church registers, academic records and electoral rolls, which at various stages has meant checking and double checking that the identity of the family member in question was correct. Even today quite often writers leave out the 'e' before the 'y' when spelling his name.

In my genealogy work on the family which has produced the family tree set out on pages 14 and 15, I discovered that it was Frederick William (see plate 2) who brought the Ketelbey name to Birmingham, when he moved here from London in the late 1820s with an aunt and his oldest sister Amelia, in order to find employment. This was at a time when the inner regional towns and cities of the land appeared to be less affected by the depression, which was more prevalent in the capital, and the young Frederick eventually found work as an apprentice in the growing jewellery trade of the thriving little town - as it was then.

He was to be the first of several of his kin to work in the famous Birmingham Jewellery Quarter, including his sons George Henry as an engraver and Frederick George of 3 Smith Street, Hockley, as a jewellery case manufacturer and plush mounter, whose own sons Frederick Benjamin George and Henry Thomas also became jewellers. Although their father Frederick George began his career in the jewellery trade, later on he took a very keen interest in photography, eventually establishing his own photographic studio in 1899 at 279 Wheeler Street, Aston Manor, being amongst the first of such studios set up in Birmingham. It was I believe his own son Frederick Benjamin George who also later took up an interest outside the jewellery trade, when in 1894 he established a specialised drapery wholesaling business at 261 Farm Street, Hockley, trading as "Frederick Ketelbey - Baby Linen Warehouse". Frederick William's daughter Ann (often called Annie) also established her own retail drapers store at 23 Key Hill, Hockley, and following her marriage to Alfred David Morgan in 1870 the couple developed the store into a thriving little business.

Like many families the Ketelbeys kept up the tradition of maintaining the same Christian names in the lineage of the family. This can be seen on the family tree, on which you will also see that the last public records I found on the Ketelbey name, were those of the deaths of Frederick George Ketelbey of Solihull (Albert's second cousin) on 20th June 1963, and his widow Lillian Mary Ketelbey on 18th June 1967. As far as I am aware there is no one of the name who now lives in the Birmingham area, nor for that matter in the rest of the United Kingdom, due to the male line of the family here becoming extinct.

In returning to the Ketelbeys of Alma Street and particularly father George (see plate 3), he was first and foremost a family man. A devoted and loving husband to his quiet and reserved wife whom he called "Sarann", and though a strict disciplinarian who did not approve of 'sparing the rod and spoiling the child', he was a trustworthy and loving figurehead to all of his children, to whom he was their example. He was a very amiable man and very easy to befriend, and despite being a disciplinarian he was much liked by children - not least for the excellent Christmas and birthday parties he would organise! Being highly skilled in many aspects of art, later on in his career he took the post of Art Master at Vittoria Street School of Art in Hockley, where earlier he had been a student. This was an independent school founded in 1901 under the control of a sub-committee formed from the two governing bodies, namely the Birmingham Municipal School of Art and the Birmingham Jewellers Association, the latter having been founded in 1887. With the close working relationship held between the Vittoria School and the Jewellery Association, it is believed that the engraving skills of George would have been an asset to his success as an art master, for he was to hold this post until retirement. As an expert in his field, from line drawing, etching on various materials, painting in oils and water colours, and wood carving to precision engraving and gold and silver smithing, George was indeed able to build up for himself an excellent living in the spheres of art and jewellery. Having worked as a jewellery designer in the partnership Ketelbey & Goodwin of 105 Vyse Street, for a time he was also designer for the well known Birmingham silversmiths Adie & Lovekin, for whom he also worked as a tester and an enameller.

Sarah Ann (see plate 4) was first and foremost a housewife, devoted to her husband and children, who without a servant (and until her daughters were old enough to help) performed all of the household chores of the day, and to George she was a further asset in the economy of the household, in making and mending all of her children's clothes, whereby in time she became an accomplished dressmaker.

By 1876 the family had moved to 93 Pope Street, Ladywood, and here on 26th February 1877 Edith Amelia Caroline was born, a sister to Florence and Albert, but who sadly died in infancy of anaemia on 4th April 1877. By 1878 the family had moved again to live at 134 Wilton Street, Aston Manor, where George and Sarah's sadness at losing their baby Edith was perhaps lessened much when on 27th November 1878 another daughter was born to them, whom they named Edith Lavinia. Her birth may have paved the way for father George and mother Sarah to decide to move to a larger house, for by 1881 they had done just that in moving a short distance to 19 William Street, Aston Manor, and where in the same street George was to set up a shop at number 58 as a jeweller specialising in lockets, trading under the name Henry Morgan Jeweller (interesting to note that his step sister Ann's married name was Morgan). On 12th April 1883 Sarah presented George with their fourth child, a brother to their other children in Harold George, and on 29th January 1886 a third son was born, Hubert Frank, but who

The Ketelbeys in Birmingham

Showing descendants from the first marriage of Frederick William Ketelbey

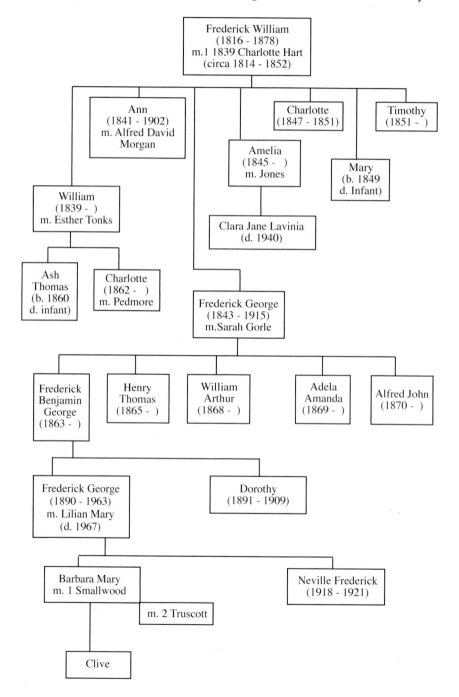

The Ketelbeys in Birmingham

Showing descendants from the second marriage of Frederick William Ketelbey

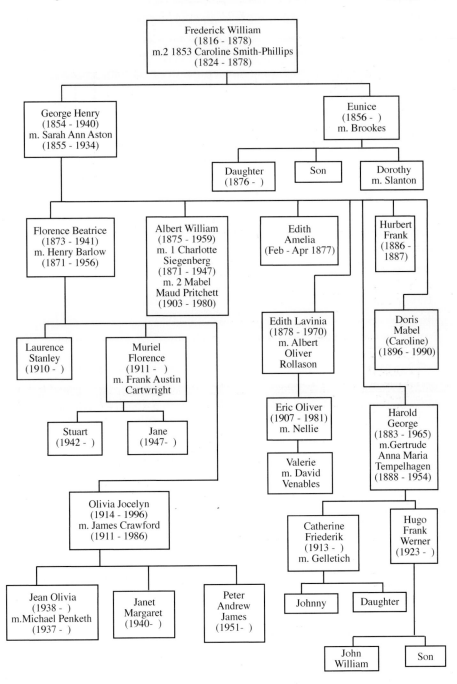

tragically died aged just 21 months on 6th November 1887 from peritonitis and bronchitis, so meaning that George and Sarah were to suffer twice the heartbreak and sadness of losing a child in infancy. Like many of George and Sarah's generation, such tragedies were very much a part of living - when circumstances of health and care were far removed from those we enjoy today - but George really did have more than his fair share of these. When he had earlier suffered the quite sudden death of his father, due to a fatal sepsis on 14th March 1878 aged 62, his was also the double tragedy of parent loss, when his broken hearted mother at just 53 years of age, also died on the day of his father's funeral.

Sad as all this was, it seemed to add to the character and resilience of George to 'get on with life', and put his full energy and enthusiasm into whatever task he was to set about doing. A commercially minded and very thrifty man (traits later very much evident in son Albert), as his work in the fields of jewellery and art began to prosper in the late 1880s, so he was able to invest money in the property market, and by the 1890s he had purchased several houses in Murdock Road in what was then the elite Handsworth area of Birmingham, for which he collected rent from the tenants. By 1894 the family itself had moved to the Handsworth area of Birmingham, into a new house purchased by George which they named "Hubertdale" in memory of their deceased little boy, which was later numbered 168 Antrobus Road.

On 4th May 1896 their family was completed when daughter Doris Mabel was born, and by 1904 they had moved again - just over the road to a much larger new house, 165 Antrobus Road[2], into the interior design of which George had incorporated a separate music room for his musical family. Here the landscaped rear garden, complete with a natural brook running at its foot, was completed to the joy of wife Sarah, and an adjacent court area to the side of the property was to be kept available, not for George (who did not drive) but for sons Albert and Harold, to park their cars there when they visited the family home. Thrifty George retained ownership of their previous home at 168 Antrobus Road[2] and by the year 1912 had also acquired ownership of number 163[2] - the adjoining property to number 165 - and these he duly rented to tenants.

Writing in March 1975, George's niece Dorothy Slanton of Sutton Coldfield (the youngest daughter of the three children of his sister Eunice) referred to her Uncle George as a remarkable man, and recalled how versatile and determined he was, "Not letting anything beat him". He was, she said, a very keen photographer (no doubt encouraged by his half-brother Frederick

---

[2] These properties, and the natural brook remain, and from the exterior are little changed (after bomb damage repairs) today.

George), and remembered that when wireless first came out, after inspecting her parents set, he made his own set including the headphones, which worked perfectly. As a child she visited 165 Antrobus Road regularly with her parents, and said her Aunt Sarah Ann was a very gentle person, whereas Uncle George was very stern, and she used to be a little frightened of him. Dorothy was of similar age to her cousin Doris, but learnt from her mother that her Uncle George was very strict with her musical cousins Albert and Harold, and any spare time had to be spent practising their music. On her visits to their father's home she was always beckoned by Uncle George to do her own practice on the family piano - whose ivory keys were worn hollow with use - whereupon, she said, she would then be criticised by him! Conversely she also went on to say how on occasions Uncle George could also be very kind and affectionate. The last time he visited her own home in Sutton Coldfield was as an old man, when her vivid memory of him in his smart attire and with his short white beard was how distinguished he looked.

George and Sarah were to remain at number 165 for the rest of their lives, Sarah dying on 12th August 1934 aged 79 years and George dying in 1940 aged 86, under rather sad circumstances. Already suffering from a weakened heart he was seriously injured when his home was bombed by enemy attack in December 1940, and was taken to the City Hospital, where he died on Christmas Day 1940. Their daughter Edith (see plate 8) was to remain a devoted and caring daughter throughout their lives, actually moving to live opposite them at 168 Antrobus Road in 1922 with her husband Albert Oliver Rollason. After his death in 1949, she stayed here until 1966, when she moved to live in the Erdington area of Birmingham with their only son, Eric Oliver William, until her own death on 5th June 1970.

Tragedy came to George and Sarah when their first-born Florence Beatrice (see plate 7) contracted scarlet fever as a baby which, although she survived, sadly rendered her deaf. She was educated at the Birmingham Deaf School where she was taught sign language, and with the help and encouragement of her mother, she later became a dress maker. In order for her to communicate with her parents and brothers and sisters, father George encouraged them all to learn sign language, which they all did to varying degrees of proficiency. In 1909 she married Henry Barlow, who was deaf and dumb from birth, and who became a much respected and liked skilled worker, and indeed apprentice trainer, at the famous Birmingham compressor makers Bellis and Morcombe. The couple set up home in Boulton Road, Handsworth, not far from George and Sarah's home, which meant that as supportive parents they were close by to give their daughter and son-in-law a hand when they were to have children of their own. Through their union

Florence and Henry produced three healthy children and from the marriage of their youngest daughter Olivia Jocylyn to James Crawford there came three grandchildren, the oldest of which is my friend Jean Olivia Penketh - and whose resemblance to her Great Uncle Albert William Ketèlbey is quite incredible! (See plate 10). A touching anecdote in Florence's misfortune was the love and devotion her father showed towards her in a very practical way. Whilst father George was quite a social animal who enjoyed dancing, his quiet wife Sarah did not. So it was that with much pride he took as his partner to Mayoral and other balls, his deaf and dumb daughter who loved dancing (see plate 11). Compared to other Ketelbeys' longevity, Florence died at a comparatively young age, just two days before her 68th birthday, on 9th December 1941.

As we shall see with brother Albert, likewise Harold George Ketelbey (see plate 6) was to prove himself somewhat of a child prodigy with his gift for music, and particularly the playing of the violin. He was to become a brilliant virtuoso, and for this reason I have dedicated a separate chapter at the end of this book covering a concise biography of his life and musical achievement.

Academic achievement within the Ketelbey family came through their youngest daughter, Doris Mabel (see plate 9). She was educated at King Edward's Grammar School, Birmingham, and in 1997 in meeting a fellow pupil of Doris in the form of the very charming and agile 100-year-old Miss Phyliss Eastgate of Sutton Coldfield, I was told that Doris was one of the brightest pupils in the school at that time. She went on to further study at Birmingham University and then Somerville College, Oxford, before holding a string of appointments as a lecturer in Modern History, culminating in her appointment in this role at St. Andrew's University, Scotland, which post she held from 1938 to 1958, being seconded for a year in 1951 to serve as Professor of Modern History at the University of the Gold Coast (now Ghana), West Africa.

The author of various text books including *A History of Modern Times*, she never married and was often called Caroline (her Grandmother's name). Following her retirement she worked occasionally as a freelance editor, and died at St. Andrew's Scotland on 14th December 1990, aged 94 years.

THE BIRMINGHAM HOMES OF
GEORGE HENRY KETELBEY AND HIS FAMILY

1873 - 1875   7 RICHMOND TERRACE, HOCKLEY.

1875 - 1877   41 ALMA STREET, ASTON MANOR.

1877 - 1878   93 POPE STREET, LADYWOOD.

1878 - 1881   134 WILTON STREET, ASTON MANOR.

1881 - 1894   19 WILLIAM STREET, ASTON MANOR.

1894 - 1904   168 ANTROBUS ROAD, HANDSWORTH.

1904 - 1941   165 ANTROBUS ROAD, HANDSWORTH.

CHAPTER 3

THE MUSIC BEGINS

Great works are performed not by strength but by perseverance.......

Anon.

*T*he music that was in George Henry's blood was without doubt passed on to at least three of his children, and indeed music was included as part of their education from the start, for all of the children, with the exception of Florence. Whereas his own aspirations to make a career in music had been denied him by his father, due to the uncertainty of continuous employment in such in mid-nineteenth century Birmingham, he was to give much encouragement to those of his kin whose musical talents were obvious to him. He enjoyed playing the violin and was very interested in the technical aspects of the instrument. This interest together with his artistic and technical abilities led him to enjoy making violins and experimenting in their construction from different woods and materials. Violins of different shapes and sizes were therefore a regular feature of their home, seen hanging from picture rails in the hall and other rooms, and several of them were said to be quite playable. Meanwhile George's musical talents were more than equalled by wife Sarah, who was herself an enthusiastic and very able amateur pianist, whose own family were said to be quite musical, being of Welsh origin. Like her mother, although she never became a professional musician, Edith Lavinia was a proficient pianist and loved playing the piano, which she did apparently quite robustly. She played and practised regularly and well into old age, and loved the family tradition of "home concerts" which she continued to encourage in her own home on many a Sunday night.

Likewise younger sister Doris was taught piano, but her heart was in reading and history from a young age, and although she never became a keen pianist, her father very much enjoyed playing duets with his youngest daughter.

Harold as we shall see later made out very well in his career as a violinist, but it was of course Albert who was to prove himself the star musician of the family.

As a young boy Albert showed remarkable talent on the piano and several people have referred to him as a child prodigy. With a natural talent for singing he soon became head chorister at St. Silas' Church (see plates 15 & 16), St. Silas' Square, Church Street,Lozells (built in 1854) just around the corner from the Aston Wesleyan Chapel, in Lozells Road, where in 1874 several members had formed a football club, which was later to become known as Aston Villa. At St. Silas' he was quite often called upon to sing solos, and his proud mother encouraged him much in this, and indeed in his piano playing, being such a keen pianist herself. It was his father, however, who arranged for him to have private lessons with a Mr. W. Newey, and who set his own rigorous time table of piano practice - not always, it should be hastened to add, to the pleasure of the young boy! W. Newey was a member of a family who were friends of father George and who were very much involved in the art world, and Albert's youngest sister Doris, when writing about him in later life said, "Like my father, W. Newey treated both music and art as very serious matters", being, she said, "A splendid person who gave my father much dedicated service". - to the obvious benefit of his young student Albert.

With a family of four young children to rear, things were far from easy for George and Sarah. Though George was a skilled worker, like others of their generation the family had to live on a tight budget, and when necessity demanded, had to use the services of the most popular finance houses of the time - the pawnbroker. In the last quarter of the nineteenth century Mrs. Emma Green ran her family's Pawnbroker's shop at 139 Farm Street, Hockley, and among the stories of her exploits, which have been passed down through the family, was one her grandson George Henry (Harry) Green[3] told me. This was of Sarah Ann Ketelbey being a frequent customer at the shop, pawning the family piano on a 'retained possession ticket', in order to pay for young Albert's piano lessons.

Following local primary school education, possibly at St. Silas' Church of England School[4], (established 1852) or Alma Street County Primary School[4] (established 1878), by the age of 11 he was one of the first music students of the newly formed School of Music (now the Birmingham Conservatoire) of the Birmingham and Midland Institute[5] combining here his continuing formal education. Under the tutorship of Dr. A. R. Gaul

---

[3] Harry Green was born in 1925 at 18 Gerrard Street (just opposite the author's birth place). He now lives at Shenstone, Staffordshire, and as a keen amateur violinist is leader of Walsall Senior Citizens Orchestra, who regularly include the music of Ketèlbey in their monthly concerts at Walsall Town Hall.

[4] Unfortunately archive registers of attendance at local schools for this period no longer exist.

[5] The Birmingham and Midland Institute had been founded by Act of Parliament in 1854, "For the Diffusion and Advancement of Science, Literature and Art amongst all Classes of Persons resident in Birmingham and the Midland Counties".

(composition) and Dr. H. W. Wareing (harmony), the boy progressed well in his music studies, and by the age of 12 excelled in musical harmony, as the 1888 examination results of the school shown on page 23 prove. It is therefore difficult to believe that by his own admission, he was 'a reluctant child pianist', but was inspired to play and compose by a passion for the daughter of the organist as St. Silas' - perhaps even at this early age a romantic!

In the year 1888 a substantial report was drawn up covering the great diversity of activities within the Birmingham and Midland Institute, and the School of Music, then just two years old, was asked to contribute to this report. Dr. H. W. Wareing who taught harmony thus reported. "On the whole the work as class work, was satisfactory both in the Advanced and Elementary divisions; the paper of Albert W. Ketelbey being exceptionally praiseworthy."

It was no doubt the fine tuition and influence of his teacher of composition, Dr. A. R. Gaul, which went some way to enable the boy to write his first serious piece of music - *Sonata for Pianoforte* (see plate 14), composed in late 1888 when he was just 13 years of age. Some previous writers have said that the boy Ketelbey played this sonata at a concert at Worcester Town Hall before an admiring young Edward Elgar (1857 - 1934) later Sir Edward Elgar, who was in the audience. In my own enquiries of archive files at Worcester City Library and the Elgar Birthplace Museum, in trying to pin-point an exact date for this, I found no mention of such a concert appearance. As one so gifted at such a young age, he could of course have been asked to make a special guest performance at such a concert, without there being any recorded mention of it. Ketelbey's youngest sister Doris certainly knew of this story, but according to her, he regarded it as irrelevant and unimportant, and indeed she remembered that when it was once mentioned to him in later life, the only response it brought from him was a derisory smile!

In 1889 his parents wanted him to enter the Royal College of Music in London, but having just missed the date of entry for a scholarship to that college, they encouraged him to compete for the three-year Queen Victoria Scholarship for Composition at Trinity College of Music, London, which he won at still only 13 years of age, coming out many marks above the other entrants and even beating the composer Gustav Holst, who came second. A special prize from his parents for this achievement was to be a fully bound volume of Mozart Piano Sonatas, complete with a beautiful front cover plate designed and drawn by his father. Later, as a man he was to write in pencil across the title of the *No. 16 - C Major Sonata* the words "Murdered into a Jazz - In an eighteenth century drawing room". So it was, on 27th

THE BIRMINGHAM AND MIDLAND INSTITUTE
School of Music - 1888 Results.

CLARIONET, ELEMENTARY.........2nd class)Pick, W.J.
)Peach, A.E.
One Candidate failed

CLARIONET, ADVANCED.............1st class Gabb, W. Watkin
2nd class)Matthewson, James H.
)Sharp, George A.
Three Candidates failed

FLUTE & PICCOLO,ELEMENTARY....2nd class)Timmins, Frank
)Lees, F.
)Terry, S.
Two Candidates failed

FLUTE & PICCOLO, ADVANCED......................)1st class   Ensor, Charles
)2nd class   Payne, Walter
One Candidate failed

HARMONY, ELEMENTARY...........1st class Cuthbertson, Emily M.
2nd class)Eadie, Charles G.
)Field, Edward
)Prosser, Arthur H.
)Johnson, Florence S.
)Johnson, Alice
)Hackett, Henry
Five Candidates failed

HARMONY, ADVANCED..................1st class Ketelbey, Albert W.
...2nd class)Blackwell, Elizabeth
)Gaul, Ethel M.
)Morton, Linda
)Leather, Annie E.
)Trobridge, Bessie
Three Candidates failed

June 1889 Articles of Pupilship were signed up with Trinity College of Music, and as a teenager he went off to London life where he was to continue his formal education at Fitzroy College, Fitzroy Square, and his musical one under G. E. Bambridge (piano) and Dr. G. Saunders (composition and harmony) at Trinity.

It was not long, however, before he was back in Birmingham! As a boarder at Fitzroy College his fear of the stick-bearing lame headmaster there, who it was said 'would beat with his stick any unruly boys', was too much for him to bear, and within just a few weeks of his first term he persuaded the cook to lend him some money, with which he duly purchased a railway ticket and returned home to mom and dad! After some consolation his father took him back, only for the same escapade to happen again later! Following this his father decided that it would be better if he could stay in "approved lodgings", which is what happened when he moved to the home of a Mr. & Mrs. Alfred Hoare and their musical family at 8 Queen Square, Bloomsbury, WC1. This settled the score for young Albert because he loved it here, and particularly liked their daughter Miss Florence. She was a talented song writer who was to later write the words to thirty-seven of Ketelbey's early songs, including the first four of twelve lyrical pieces he had published between 1902 and 1905. The stick-bearing headmaster had, however, made an impression upon Albert, which was to remain with him for the rest of his life, for whenever he recalled his generally happy memories of college, this man was 'the fly in the ointment' and he always referred to him as "The Brute and Barbarian". As dark an impression as this may have been, it was in no way to influence Albert's own way of dealing with people in later life - in fact quite the reverse - as in all his dealings with subordinates his hallmark was to be kindness.

He had a keen interest in modern languages and it is said that whilst at college and when settled back in his happier lodgings, he made full use of facilities there to further his education in this sphere. This interest in the study of languages was to remain with him for life, and in effect became a hobby, whereby later he was to become competent in speaking French, Italian and German. Meanwhile at Trinity he was always seen as a 'model' student, and besides studying composition under Dr. Gordon Saunders, he also studied a wide selection of instruments. Of these, he reached a professional level on piano and organ, was proficient on cello and horn and had a playing acquaintance of flute, oboe and clarinet. His favourite instrument was the cello, but it was upon the piano that his natural talent shone through.

The influence of father George must have helped young Master Albert to overcome his reluctancy, for from a young age he encouraged his son to perform in public and to seize every opportunity which came to him. This can be seen in the fact that at a private concert held at Barford Road Board Schools, Birmingham on 16th August 1889, which was organised by the Bourne family[6], Master Albert then aged 14 and whilst on his first summer vacation from college, performed two piano pieces. Likewise when back at college he was encouraged in performing publicly as part of his musical development, and as a solo pianist in his early teen years appeared at several concerts in London, besides being a regular solo performer at Trinity College concerts.

At the age of 16 in 1892 he won again the same scholarship he had won three years previously, and during the same year was appointed organist at St. John's Church, Wimbledon (built 1875), a permanent post he was to hold for some four years, combining his playing there with his continuing music composition and educational studies (see plates 17, 18 & 19). At just 16 years of age, he was one of the youngest organists of the time to take up such a responsible post. During his time as organist at St. John's he was to write church music, and several anthems including *Every Good Gift*, *Behold! Upon the Mountains*, and *Be Strong! All ye People*, and for one of these anthems it is said that he won a prize.

Whilst at Trinity he completed several compositional exercises including a *String Quartet*, a *Wind and Piano Quintet*, a *Concertstück for Piano and Orchestra*, a *Caprice for Piano and Orchestra*, an *Overture* and a *Piano Concerto in G Minor*, all of which were to be performed at London and provincial concerts. One critic, H. W., who heard him play the above mentioned *Concertstück* during a concert given by Trinity College of Music, said of it, "I was greatly struck by its attractive themes and the interesting scoring". For both composition and playing abilities he won a string of prizes and gold and silver medals. In 1890 he won the Turner Pianoforte Medal, in 1892 the College Medals for Harmony and Counterpoint and the Gabriel Prize, following which by passing further examinations he became first an Associate and later Licentiate of Trinity College of Music, when in 1895 he won the Tallis Gold Medal for the highest marks of the year in counterpoint. One prize he did not win at Trinity was for sight-reading - later in life cheerfully admitting, "I turned the music over so smartly - the lot fell down!"

Without doubt these achievements and prizes must have brought the young Ketelbey much encouragement, and his parents much pride, but what must have been "the icing on the cake" was his winning of the coveted Sir Michael Costa Prize for his *Quintet for Oboe, Clarinet, Bassoon, Horn*

---

6 The Bourne family at this time owned and ran their own engineering company in Birmingham, and it is believed that George and Sarah Ann Ketelbey were friends of the family.

and Piano, which also won him the College Gold Medal. Michael Angus Costa (1808 - 1884) was an Italian musician who in 1827 at the age of 21 came to England, where he stayed and rose to become one of the most respected conductors of his day. As a pioneer of the modern conducting technique (i.e. standing alone on a rostrum in front of the orchestra) he played a significant part in putting Birmingham on the "musical map", particularly through his involvement in the Birmingham Triennial Musical Festivals, becoming conductor of the Festival in 1849, which post he held until 1882. The fact that Costa had such a close relationship with the city must have intensified the family's pleasure when Albert won this prize.

The young Mr. Ketelbey's mind now seemed set upon becoming a composer of 'serious' music and combined with his writing of music for the church, he had also published under his own name several short pieces, one being the beautiful *Rêverie* (dedicated to his father) for piano and another being a *Romance for piano and violin (or cello)*, which he dedicated to his adopted London mother - Mrs. Alfred Hoare. Other songs and lighter pieces for piano and mandolin, he published under the pseudonym Raoul Clifford, in order to conceal and reserve his real name for other serious compositions to follow. It is interesting to note that 'Clifford' Street was a residential thoroughfare just around the corner from the Alma Street of his birth, and which remains to this day, and this could possibly have been the basis of the name.

As regards his real name, he had by now started to enter an accent over the second 'e' of the Ketelbey name, as he apparently hated being referred to as KETTLEBEY (i.e. the first syllable pronounced as the boiling recep-tacle) and by entering the accent, this pointed to the emphasis being put on a second syllable i.e. Ke-TEL-bey when it was pronounced, besides adding a foreign air to the name. His brother Harold soon followed this same ploy in his own career.

By this time he had established himself as a pianist of some ability appearing at concerts in London, notably at the Queen's Hall and the Prince's Hall, and in provincial towns and cities, including his home town Birmingham. On 8th June 1896 Trinity College, who took much pride in the success of their student, included an *Orchestral Suite in Three Movements* recently composed by Ketèlbey, in a packed concert at the Queen's Hall given by students of the college under the baton of Mr. F. Corder. This serious piece was reported as receiving much acclaim from the audience, and in *The British Musician* of December 1896, Ketèlbey was to be noted as,

> "One of the most promising of our young composers......whose melodies are flowing and rhythmical......so later we may expect some important orchestral works from his pen."

Barford Road Board Schools,

AUGUST 16th, 1889.

M.C. - - MR. W. H. TYE.

MARCH - - - - Master A. KETTELBY.
POLKA ....
SONG - - - - Mr. JAMES BOURNE.
QUADRILLE ....
NEGRO ENTERTAINMENT Mr. C. LUTON.
VALSE ....
SONG - - - - Mr. FRANK PEARSON.
LANCERS ....
SONG - - - - Mr. W. PEARSON.
PIANOFORTE SOLO - Master A. KETTELBY.
SONG - - - - - Miss H. HILLITT.
SONG - - - - Mr. T. BOURNE, Sen.
SCHOTTISCHE ....

INTERVAL.

VALSE...
SONG - - - - - Mrs. H. BOURNE.
SONG - - - - - Mr. F. PEARSON.
MAZURKA...
SONG - - - - - Mr. JOHN BOURNE.
SONG - - - - - Mr. W. BOURNE.
QUADRILLE ....
SONG - - - - - Mr. H. BOURNE.
SIR ROGER DE COVERLEY.

" We are a Merry Family."

Programme for concert held at Barford Road Board Schools, in which
Master Albert performed two piano pieces.

With acknowledgement Lawrence Wrigley.

However, his musical talents had already been seized upon by the variety theatre world when he had been offered the post of conductor by the manager of a travelling light opera company, who were about to commence a tour of a musical comedy. It is reported that in response to this job offer the young Ketèlbey replied in all honesty, "But I don't know anything about conducting", to which his prospective boss replied (perhaps unknowingly - quite prophetically) "Never mind about that, you'll soon find out how!"

At such a young and impressionable age he must have seen this opportunity to work as a conductor as a great honour, and although not in the sphere of serious music, he gladly accepted it. Relinquishing his posts at Trinity College and at St. John's, he went on tour with much enthusiasm, and his natural talent and apparent 'air of command' as a conductor was soon to be seen by all. Although he left his post at St. John's Church, he remained a keen organist, and it is believed that for a further twelve months or so, when it was opportune he would from time to time continue to play there. In later years his work with Trinity College was to continue when he was appointed a main board examiner, but even as early as 1896, in his role as Licentiate, he had already served the college as an examiner in harmony for local examinations connected with the college. Maybe this theatre post was destiny's first hand to detract him from his serious career, for his success in his conductor role was such that following a tour of some two years he was immediately appointed Musical Director of the Opera Comique[7] in the Strand, at just 22 years of age the youngest theatrical conductor in London.

This achievement, however, did not please father George who had not approved of his son's first appointment as a travelling conductor. George's intent in all he had done for Albert was for him to make a career in the arena of serious music, and he viewed the theatre as being a far remove from the expectations he had for his son. Perhaps George used the opportunity to take his son to task about this, when occasionally, "In Albert's bachelor days", as Doris Ketelbey put it, "he and my father would 'hop over' to Paris, where my father had once worked in a studio for a short time, to look at the Louvre or some Exposition". It may well have been that by this time young Albert was keen, even impatient, to establish his independence, and therefore saw his theatre posts as enabling him to achieve such, however, it is believed that this variance of vision with his father was to sadly mar forever the relationship between them. Interestingly, one unconfirmed report speaks of Ketèlbey actually playing in theatre bands "on the quiet" whilst still at Trinity College, which if true would provide the

7 The Opera Comique was later demolished to make way for the development of the Aldwych.

logical reason for the manager of the travelling light opera company being aware of his talents, but which, if his father had known, would only have intensified his disapproval of his son's antics!

He moved into his new home in London at 13 Bruton Street[8], just yards away from the famous Berkeley Square, and just a few doors away from number 17 where our own Queen Elizabeth II was to be born some twenty six years later. With his appointment at the Opera Comique came the immediate opportunity to compose and arrange musical comedy selections, music for plays, pantomime and the like. Ironically it could well have been when working at the Opera Comique, that after writing a piece of background music depicting a river scene in a music hall sketch, that he was told by an admiring colleague, "This is rather above the average of the stuff we get here, you really ought to try and write some serious works!"

Even though increasingly involved in his theatre work, he maintained his interest in serious music and his association with Trinity College, as on 23rd June 1898 when he gave a recital of several of his serious compositions at the college, including his prize winning *Piano Quintet*, and other pieces for violin and for flute. Included amongst several of his songs *Blow! blow! thou winter wind* (words by William Shakespeare from *As You Like It*) was sung by his friend and fellow composer Giuseppi Villa. Villa was in the main a composer of songs, for whom interestingly Florence Hoare also wrote many of the words, and for one of his songs *A Dream of Glory*, Ketèlbey had previously written an organ obbligato under his pseudonym Raoul Clifford. Later in 1899 Ketèlbey was to have a song published, with words by Charles Kingsley, entitled *The Knight's Return*, and this he dedicated 'To my friend G. Villa'.

In his new role at the Opera Comique he was soon to be actively involved in what was to be an enormous success, when they put on a pantomime version of *Alice in Wonderland* which played to packed audiences from December 1898 to March 1899, and for which the young Ketèlbey possibly wrote some of the music. It is interesting to note that later in 1907 Ketèlbey had published a serious work entitled *Alice in Wonderland - Four characteristic pieces for Piano*, but whether these were adaptations of some of the music he had written for this pantomime I do not know. However, what followed *Alice in Wonderland* was a very different story in terms of theatrical success.

Skipped by the Light of the Moon was a musical comedy which had had its birth in America back in the 1880s when two Americans, using the George Sims farce *A Gay City* as its story line, produced the musical

---

8 This end of Bruton Street was destroyed by German bombs in the Second World War, the current four storey building of 13 Bruton Street now being used as commercial offices.

version as *Skipped by the Light of the Moon* and which had a successful American tour for some ten years. In 1896 the comedian George Walton was able to secure the rights to produce it in the United Kingdom, and after Walton had updated the work to bring the comedy in line with topical and British sense of humour, a first British performance in Reading in August 1896 heralded the start of a series of provincial tours which had much success. By 1899 the musical comedy had not yet been produced in London, and in discovering that George Walton was in preparation for another provincial tour, the management of the Opera Comique were able instead to persuade him to put it on in the capital for the first time, as a follow on to the success of *Alice in Wonderland.*

It was decided to produce the London work under the title *A Good Time*, and in line with other variety musicals of the time, its nature and versatility of story line meant that existing songs could be altered or dropped and/or new and popular songs and musical pieces inserted, or substituted for others, as was felt necessary, and this in turn provided the opportunity for the Musical Director of the new London production "to shine". Ketèlbey therefore both arranged and wrote musical selections and songs, including his songs *There's something in the English after all!*, *Under the Starlight* and *In Sweet Disguise*, but sadly the show, which had had so much success in the provinces, was not sophisticated enough for London audiences, and after opening at the Opera Comique in April 1899, following poor reviews, by May 1899 it was all over!

Unfortunately the losses incurred due to the failure of *A Good Time* were to bankrupt the proprietors of the Opera Comique, and the theatre was never used again, so ending young Mr. Ketèlbey's job there. After the success of *Alice in Wonderland*, the disappointment and sadness in being part of this sudden failure would have been worse for Albert were it not for the fact that during his work at the Opera Comique he had met a young attractive and rather petite actress and soprano singer in the form of Miss Lottie Siegenberg - who some years later was to become his wife. Such was Albert's leaning towards her, that in having published his song *In Sweet Disguise*, it bore the caption:-

Dedicated to and sung by
MISS LOTTIE SIEGENBERG
With the greatest success in the Musical Comedy
"Skipped by the Light of the Moon".

Whether it was his sheer optimism for the success of *A Good Time*, or the fact that the song really was a success in its short life on the London stage, or whether it was just a part of his advances in trying to win the charms of the young lady that led him to refer to the song as a success, is not known. What is known of course is the fact that he wisely credits it to *Skipped by the Light of the Moon*, and it could well be that this, and indeed those other pieces he wrote for the work, were included in the same musical comedy when it continued its tours of the more receptive provinces under its old title. Meanwhile, Lottie, who loved the theatre, was to make regular appearances on the London comic opera scene, being particularly successful in a comic opera entitled *The Fisher Girl*, written and composed by Oscar Brand and William Gliddon (the latter being the Musical Director of the Grand Theatre, Islington), which was to have two tour runs in 1901, and following its popularity and success was to have a further spring run in 1903.

Even at the age of 23 Ketèlbey had that fortitude which was to remain an integral part of his character, for he was soon to put the disappointment of the Opera Comique behind him, and press on with the opportunity of earning what he could in variety theatre land, and by the year 1900 had written the music for a comic opera in the style of Gilbert and Sullivan - *The Wonder Worker*, which appeared in the same year at the Grand Theatre, Fulham. Although the story line and wit in this were not seen as a success, *The Stage* described Ketèlbey's music as being "....well written lyrics set to tuneful, sparkling and lively music....." Such praise of his ability no doubt seemed to confirm his penchant for the theatre, and together with his previous experience, went some way to help him secure conducting work with other provincial and West End theatres. The next decade, however, could not have been an easy one for him to achieve success in the theatre. Although the failure of the Opera Comique was not of his making, it must have been a heavy cross to bear - even a stigma - in having been so closely associated with it in musical terms, but Albert's fortitude meant he was determined. As such he was prepared to plod on and take whatever theatre work he could, both in London and the provinces, and do it with his full energy and enthusiasm, without fuss or glory. He combined this with a busy schedule of publishing work and from 1907 a busy schedule of recording work with a famous record company - both aspects of which I will cover in more detail in the next chapter.

Meticulous and somewhat of a stickler for efficiency and punctuality (traits inherited from his father) he had an infectious enthusiasm, however, and was always courteous and good humoured, the latter virtues making him a very likeable character with whom fellow professionals liked working.

Although as a man he was not of large physical stature, from an early age Ketèlbey had a large, generous but humble heart, which came to light in many aspects of his life, as we shall see. He drew much pleasure from treating the members of the orchestras he conducted to a drink at the end of a performance, a kind habit which probably started in these early theatre days, in knowing first hand what it was like for those musicians who had to earn their living in the hot pits of theatres. As his fame and personal wealth were to grow, so too was his generosity in privately helping financially those less fortunate than himself, and indeed in contributing significantly and regularly to the Musicians Benevolent Fund from the time of its founding in 1921.

In appearance he was a short man about five feet five inches in height (noted to have particularly short legs), blessed with a good crown of dark wavy hair, brushed back and neatly parted in the middle, and bespectacled from a young age (thought to be his early 20s), and in spite of his short stature he was smart in appearance, and even as a young man always carried an air of elegance and distinction, which were to remain with him for the rest of his life.

CHAPTER 4

TO COLUMBIA AND INTO THE PICTURES

Low brow my music may well be,
But it's livened the scenes,
On silent film screens,
And what's wrong with that, will you tell me?

Albert W. Ketèlbey.

$\mathcal{R}$egardless of his father's disappointment with him, from the time Albert entered the theatre world his indigenous desire for serious musician-ship remained with him, and from about 1900 he was able to absorb himself more in this genre when he began working for the music publishing company Hammond & Co., who had up to then published most of his compositions. Here his main task was to be making arrangements of solo piano pieces and full orchestral pieces for small orchestras, i.e. palm court and municipal orchestras, which were a growing medium of entertainment at this time. He also transcribed full orchestral pieces for solo piano, and much of this work for Hammond & Co. included many classical pieces by such as Beethoven, Tchaikovsky, Chopin, Mendelssohn and Schuman. In 1904 he also undertook the transcription of various works of pantomime and theatre for piano, for the music publisher Chappell & Co., and in 1910 the transcription of various piano works for orchestra for the music publisher Elkin & Co. This publishing work was said to be invaluable "hands on" experience which contributed significantly to the fluency of his composition ability. Between 1903 and 1907 he was kept particularly busy by Hammond & Co. and Chappell & Co. in doing an assortment of revising, arranging and editing, and he was to continue to work for Hammond & Co. and Elkin & Co. from time to time in this capacity right through to the 1920s. From his pen there came more compositions, including several piano works - impromptus, waltzes and mazurkas and duets for piano with various other instruments; also organ music, anthems, sacred and other serious songs, along with other lighter love songs, comedy songs and musical arrangements for the pantomime, music hall and theatre arena. These compositions included his *Six Musical Impressions for Piano, Scherzo de Concert for Flute and Piano, Prelude in C Sharp Minor* and the songs *The Heavenly Message, Kildoran, My Heart A-dream* and *The Hearts Awakening.*

True romance must have had an impression upon the character of some of this music, for having eventually courted the previously mentioned Lottie Siegenberg the happy couple were married at St. Giles Register Office, London on 27th August 1906, at which her oldest brother Louis, his wife Alice (nèe Hay) and Lottie's youngest sister Leah were main signature witnesses, and following which they settled down into married life at 42 (Upper) Bedford Place[9], Bloomsbury, London. The newly wed husband was heartily welcomed into the large Siegenberg family, in which he was to become a favourite "Uncle Albert" to those children born to Lottie's brothers and sisters, and the wider Siegenberg family. Meantime, Lottie was to prove to be of much larger and livelier character than her petite frame tended to imply, and as Albert's constant companion she was to become the source of much of his encouragement, although at the same time to some she was to appear to be somewhat domineering over him, as we shall see later.

Lottie (full maiden name Charlotte Rachael Alexandria Siegenberg) was born on 19th November 1871 at 4 Albany Place, Ratcliff, East London, the eldest of three daughters and four sons born to Lewis Siegenberg and his wife Charlotte (nèe Renshaw). Father Lewis was himself one of a large closely knit and wealthy Jewish family of German extraction, who like his relations John, Michael, Jacob and Henry, was to make his fortune in the furniture business. Other relatives of Lewis were involved in an assortment of lucrative enterprises, e.g. the clothing business (Solomon and Jacob), artist brush manufacturing (Charles), cigar making (Israel) and boot making (Samuel). By 1880 the Siegenberg family of Lewis and Charlotte had moved to the Islington district of London, eventually settling at 121 Highbury New Park[10], Islington, which was to remain a family home well into the last century, and it was probably the connotations of the First World War, which led to certain members of the Siegenberg family changing their surname

Lottie's brother Louis for example decided to adopt his father's first name, and so became Louis Lewis, and he perhaps epitomised how much the family were to become liked and respected in the Islington neighbourhood, when later in 1922, by which time he had his own antiques furniture business and was living in the family home, he was elected a councillor for St. Mary's ward on Islington Borough Council, in which he was to be elected Mayor for the year 1925/26 (see plate 21), and by which time he was also a Justice of the Peace. Sadly soon after his election as Mayor he was

---

9 This property remains to this day, from the exterior, as it was then.
10 This property remains to this day, from the exterior, as it was then (see plate 22).

to suffer the bereavement of his wife Alice, but fortunately he was able to depend upon the support of his own large family of four sons and two daughters, and his daughter Irene was to fulfil the role of Mayoress for the duration of his term as Mayor. Louis was renowned as a man of both verve and kindness in all of his affairs, virtues which were very much akin to his brother-in-law Albert, and possibly the reason why the composer was to become so close to him and his descendants. Lottie's brother Michael was to marry Constance Mary Young, and to them on 18th May 1907 at their home at 39 Douglas Road, Islington, was born Clifford Michael Siegenberg. Michael, who was a master house furnisher, decided to change his surname to Curzon, and so the boy became known as Clifford Michael Curzon, and later as the famous international concert pianist Sir Clifford Curzon (1907 - 1982) (see plate 20).

In reminiscing during an interview with Alan Blyth for *The Gramophone* in May 1971, Sir Clifford said that he thought that his father had hoped that he would follow in his Uncle Albert's footsteps in making his fortune in the field of composition, and that his first musical memory was that of sitting on the top step of the staircase listening to his Uncle Albert trying out his compositions on the piano downstairs, after supposedly having been put to bed by his nurse in the top floor bedroom of their Islington home!

For all of his endeavours a very real break came for Ketèlbey in 1907, when providence paved the way for the beginning of a long and happy association with the Columbia Graphophone Company Ltd.[11] He was engaged initially as their "impresario", but after a short time an incident arose within the studio which enabled him to make swift progress with Columbia. This happened when an Italian opera singer was recording a song, but was far from happy with the orchestral accompaniment, for which he blamed the regular conductor of the studio orchestra, and so Ketèlbey was asked if he would try his hand at satisfying the artists orchestral requirements. His acquaintance with the Italian language must have been a godsend here, for having completed a successful recording - and to the satisfaction of the singer - he was then offered this conducting role as a permanent post, which he duly accepted, and over the years rose to become Musical Director and Advisor.

In 1907 the recording industry was very much in its infancy, and worlds apart from the microchip technology used today, which gives us our quality CD recordings. In order to get a feel as to how things in the "recording room" (as it was then called) were then, I quote below an extract

---

11 Columbia was an American company who set up its British operation in 1900, and who later in 1931 merged with The Gramophone Company Ltd. (owners of the famous HMV "Nippper the Dog" trade mark) to become Electric & Musical Industries Ltd., more commonly known to us today as EMI.

from a fascinating article which appeared in *The Gramophone* in November 1940, entitled "Behind the Needle - looking over forty years of the Gramophone". This was written by Herbert C. Ridout a colleague of Ketèlbey's at Columbia, and very much a pioneer salesman with the recording company in their early years of operation in the United Kingdom.

"The recording room - only in later years was it euphemistically described as a studio - was an interesting study by comparison with that of to-day. For all sorts of devices had to be used to focus and concentrate the artist and band upon the horn or horns connected with the recording stylus. The recording machine was in one room, the artists in another. One serious problem was to secure steady running of the wax disc on the turntable. Clock-work motors and electric motors were tried, but the pull of the stylus would often vary the speed and this, even if infinitesimal, would ruin the reproduction. Finally, the best method was found to be the simple scheme of a counter-weight, carefully adjusted, and this, like other contrivances in the recording room, remained in use right up to the coming of electric recording.

In the recording room the problem was not only enforced focusing upon the horn, but the right balance of the orchestra or band. So there were a number of small platforms of varying heights, each large enough to hold a chair and a music stand. The piano, always an upright, had its back removed. The Stroh violins were nearest the horn. Muted strings were never mentioned. The French horns, having to direct the bells of their instruments towards the recording horn, would turn their backs on it and were provided with mirrors in which they could watch the conductor. The tuba was positioned right back away from the horn and his bell turned away from it; he also watched in a mirror. The big drum never entered a recording room. For a flute obbligato the flautist would leave his seat, dash round and take his place alongside the singer, and then rush back to his stand.

For singer with orchestra, two horns would be used, sometimes more. The horns themselves were strapped lavishly with adhesive tape to kill any inherent metallic ring. All sorts and sizes and shapes of horns and different materials were tried, for each recording engineer was an earnest student in his job, bent on overcoming the difficulties and the losses incurred in the sinuous ways traversed by sound between the actual artist and the recording stylus.

The horns projected into the recording-machine room through a partition. Here, where the operators worked, was a shrine of mystery. Nobody was allowed to pass into it. It was some years before I apparently established the necessary confidence in my colleagues to be permitted to enter its portals. Yet there was not much to be seen. A turntable mounted on a heavy steel base, controlled by a gravity weight, a floating arm with its recording diaphragm. A small bench, usually strewn with spare diaphragms, and a heating cupboard where the wax blanks were slightly warmed to soften the recording surface.

Through a sliding glass panel in the partition the recorder could communicate with artists and conductor. He could be dimly seen watching the revolving disc and gently blowing away the curling spirals of wax as the recording stylus cut the sound waves. It was some years before a glass suction tube was installed as a substitute for the recorder's breath to carry off the wax shavings."

It was said that Ketèlbey had a facile method of conducting, which must have been an asset to him in the cramped conditions of the recording room in which he had to conduct - with the absolute necessity of his own silence, whereby "only by the baton" could he extract the best of his desired interpretations of the music, from those playing under him. As one old violinist who used to play for him at Columbia once said, "Mr. K knew his job and we knew ours. He picked his men carefully - no time could be wasted and there were no retakes in those days. He had no mannerisms like some conductors have nowadays". He was very popular with artists and with those musicians who worked under him (a popularity no doubt accentuated by his continuing "drinks all round afterwards" philosophy) and in the profession was always referred to as "Mr. K". This name possibly came into being not long after he arrived at Columbia, when an engineer "did the almost unforgivable" and called him "Kettleby". In response the new conductor gave the engineer a short lecture on pronunciation, which went something along the lines of "As you say King CanUTE and not CANute - so when pronouncing my name you should say KeTELbey". Probably as confused as we are reading this today - the easier solution would be "Mr. K".

He was just as popular with the 'run-of-the-mill' studio staff, as highlighted by Mr. H. D. F. Fayers who joined Columbia in 1918 as an office boy, and who had the regular job of taking cheques for artists up to the recording manager in the recording room, which in those days was on the top floor of their 98 Clerkenwell Road premises. In doing this task he would often meet Ketèlbey, and remembered him as "A dapper man, somewhat on the short side with a nice smile, and always a 'good morning' or some such remark, if he met you in the lift or in the passages". By this time Ketèlbey had become quite keen on golf, and he also remembered that often between recording sessions, he would see him practising putting with the manager in the recording room office!

In his work with Columbia he was to be involved in a wide spectrum of music. In the classical repertoire this ranged from the orchestral music of Suppé and Offenbach to Wagner and Schubert, and choral music from Bizet's *Carmen* to Handel's anthems. In the lighter repertoire from music of his own composition, besides that of his contemporaries, to the music of Gilbert and Sullivan and Gershwin. Another orchestral member - Jack Ockenden (whom I speak of more in Chapter 7) once recalled the versatility of his boss at Columbia, when he said that after recording one of the classics, he would think nothing of then accompanying someone like Harry Champion in *Any old Iron*. Referring also to his great skill as a communicator and his ability to talk to all people and get the best from them, so accomplished a musician was he, that he was able to continue talking as he composed and arranged. Likewise his linguistic talents meant that he found it comparatively easy when working with foreign artists, and it is said he could change his language 'in a flash' - almost in mid stream - without even thinking about it!

His first recording with Columbia was in fact in 1909, when as solo organist he recorded Handel's 'Hallelujah' from the *Messiah*. However, his main task was to be conducting orchestras, which in the main, and presumably as part of Columbia's marketing strategy, was the studio 'house' orchestra, but under various names according to the work involved. These included Court Symphony Orchestra (classics, including opera and some light classical), Casino Orchestra (light music, waltzes, etc.), London Repertoire Orchestra (music from operetta, shows, etc.) London Revue Orchestra (music from revues, shows, etc.) and London Dance Orchestra (dance music including jazz). He would sometimes work along side a host of famous artists, including Clara Butt, Elsa Stralia, Beatrice Lillie, Carrie Herwin, Frank Mullings and Albert Sandler, all for whom, besides conducting he would often arrange and direct orchestral accompaniments. For some unknown reason, he was not always given the credit due to him for his contribution to these recordings, as often these would be issued without mention of his name on the record label or even in catalogue listings. He also made many recordings on the Regal label (a subsidiary of Columbia) with the Regal Dance Orchestra, but also, and in the main, with The Silver Stars Band - an excellent military band who were to become very well known between 1915 and 1930. Their repertoire included some arrangements of classical music, but their real talent lay in the performance of marches and band arrangements of songs, overtures, waltzes and other pieces in the lighter idiom, by Ketèlbey and his contemporaries.

So by his mid thirties he had already led a varied and very active life in the musical world, and having immersed himself into the details as to how each aspect ran, had a commercial awareness that was to both help him and grow as new opportunities came his way. Now the proud owner and driver of a motor car, he had moved home with wife Charlotte to 73 West Cromwell Road,[12] Kensington. By this time the world had not yet heard those descriptive picturesque and romantic melodies, with a character all of their own, and for which he would become famous, but the first taste of such came in 1912 when he wrote the delightful *Phantom Melody* for cello, which he dedicated to his brother Harold. For this he won a competition offered by Auguste Van Biene (see plate 23), a famous Dutch cellist of theatre and music hall of the time, which was supplemented by a £50.00 prize sponsored by *Tit-Bits*.

The idea behind Van Biene's competition was to obtain a companion piece to play alongside his own *Broken Melody* which had made him famous, and the result was that *The Phantom Melody* was unanimously chosen by Van Biene and his committee of cello experts, as being the best of over one thousand entries. Following its inaugural performance by Van Biene on 15th February 1912, at a National Sunday League Concert at the London Palladium, it soon became more popular than Van Biene's original piece. Ketèlbey orchestrated his 'winner' with brilliant effect, and words by Harold Simpson to make it a song entitled *I loved you more than I knew* (see plate 24) also added to its popularity, with it even being used as the incidental music to a London play of the same name. Ketèlbey said of the piece, "This proved a great and lasting success, and brought my name before the public in a way that had never been possible before". On his own confession he had struggled for years to gain recognition as a composer of music with a popular appeal, and he believed that it was *The Phantom Melody*

---

12 This property was demolished some years ago in a road widening scheme of West Cromwell Road.

which brought him full recognition as such, and it still remains today amongst his most popular compositions. As happy as he was with this reception which was to become a crossroads in the path of his career, if there was to be a "fly in the ointment", it was because, unfortunately father George did not apparently rejoice with his son, as again this was not of the arena of serious music, for which he believed his oldest son was able and destined.

The story of Auguste Van Biene's own rise to fame is quite incredible, when as an unknown cellist he was hungry and out of work, he decided to try his hand as a busker on the streets of London. So impressed were passers by with the brilliance and enchantment of his playing, that he was able to sustain himself with the money thrown into his cap during his first day, and so decided to continue playing as a busker. After a few days he went into Hanover Square, and having just finished playing a piece, he was approached by a gentleman, who having asked him why he was playing on the streets, gave him his business card and told him to call and see him. The card bore the name Michael Costa (previously referred to in Chapter 3) and following an interview Van Biene was engaged in the Covent Garden Orchestra. This led to him receiving engagements as a soloist in several Promenade Concerts and within a few years he was reckoned to be one of the leading cellists in London.

He then ventured into the world of comic operas, first in the early 1880s as a very successful musical director and then later in 1891, after purchasing the performing rights to several comic operas, as a very talented actor. His great love of playing the cello, however, remained with him, and his heart's desire was to have a drama written in which his beloved instrument would play a significant part.

This became a reality in 1893 with *The Broken Melody*, a comedy drama which tells the story of how a struggling musician and composer - Paul Borinski - suddenly finds success with one of his compositions. He rushes home to tell his wife the good news, but on discovering that she is out, and in his excitement, he plays the beautiful *Broken Melody*. Near its conclusion he suddenly realises that his wife has left him a note and immediately ceases his performance to read it. Through the bad influence of another woman, he discovers that she has deserted him, leaving him deeply distressed, and although success now brings him wealth and the company of many distinguished friends, he remains a sad man. Throughout the story line he performs several pieces on the cello, but it is not until the finale of the play, when after a serious illness, as a weary, worn and disappointed man that he plays *The Broken Melody* in its entirety, at the end of which his wife - who has seen the light - falls into his arms!!

The Broken Melody play became a phenomenal success for Van Biene, and by 1896 had been performed nearly 900 times the length and breadth of the country, by which time its main theme had become a very popular piece of music in its own right. Another story tells of Van Biene using it in a sketch in which he depicted a poor, starving old cellist playing, at the end of which the old cellist, whilst still playing collapses and dies. The real sadness comes in the fact that this became a reality for Auguste Van Biene, when the great character collapsed and died whilst playing on the stage of the Brighton Hippodrome in 1913.

The Phantom Melody was to arouse the interest of several publishers in this "new" Ketèlbey music, and it is perhaps interesting to note here that when some experts have analyzed his music, they have reported hearing within it the styles of other famous composers. These include Chopin and Rachmaninov in several of his serious piano pieces, and Elgar, Ives, Puccini and even Messiaen in some of his orchestral pieces.

A little 'icing on the cake' in the way of prizes, came again for Ketèlbey when at a concert at the London Hippodrome on the 23rd November 1913, his song for male voices *My Heart Still Clings to You* won the first prize of £100.00 in the competition offered by the *Evening News*, and where his song for female voices in the same competition came second. His winning song is a typical tragical-love ballad of this time, and its almost Victorian sentimentality comes through in its words as shown on page 43.

By the time of his breakthrough with *The Phantom Melody* there had appeared on the scene another arena, which was to bring him additional income. Between 1910 and 1930 cinemas were to be built, or suitable properties converted, at a phenomenal rate all over the country, and indeed the world. In Birmingham alone the number of cinemas grew from seven in 1911 to fifty three in 1916, and by the mid 1920s there were to be over 2500 cinemas throughout the land!

From the onset of silent films shown in these cinemas there was a need for what was called "atmospheric" or "mood-setting" music, played by piano, trio or small orchestra, to accompany the scenes being played out on the screen. Indeed as this new phenomenon was to grow, so large cinema "theatres" were to be built in London and other principal cities at home and abroad, and these were to employ what almost amounted to full concert orchestras. With his natural talent having already been applied to writing similar music for the theatre, Ketèlbey excelled at being able to meet the demand for this music, and was to write many pieces for this purpose.

A set of these pieces for piano was first published by Hammond & Co. in 1915, under the title *"Kinema Music"*, which bore such sub-titles as

Quiet River Scene - Love - Romance; *Pathetic - Relating to a Sad story, etc*; and *Mexican or Spanish*. In 1916 Bosworth & Co. incorporated in their *"New Moving Picture Book"* of 27 piano pieces, 22 of Ketèlbey's compositions of silent movie music, with such sub-titles as *Plaintive, Oriental Music, Hurry Music* and *Mysterioso*. This issue of Ketèlbey's pieces by Bosworth & Co. was to be revised and re-issued by them in 1924 under the new title of *"Bosworth's Loose Leaf Film - Play Music Series"* (Books 1 and 2) and in 1925 (Book 3), then representing 18 pieces with revised sub-titles, e.g. *True Love, Arabian Nights, Agitato furioso* and *Mysterious*. At the same time Bosworth & Co. issued all of these pieces under the same title in full orchestral versions, and with the piano versions this music was soon being played in cinemas all over the world. It has been said that it was the challenge of writing such music for the silent movies, which was to feed Ketèlbey's propensity to write "and paint" his masterpieces to follow, and indeed sections and fragments of several pieces of his early silent movie music, were to be later adapted and recycled as parts of his fuller orchestral picture compositions.

The publication of several of these larger orchestral "picture" works was in time to compound his success in the era of silent movies, as these (or parts of them) were to be much used in this sphere, with no adverse effects at all upon their success in the wider musical world. This use was particularly so in the case of those full orchestras of the cinema "theatres" which were to come into being, for whom the sheet music of these works was to be available "off the shelf", and as Ketèlbey also set most of these for solo piano and a selection of instrument ensembles, meant that these arrangements in sheet music form would also be readily available to those smaller combinations of musicians employed in the average and smaller sized cinemas of the provinces.

In his biographical notes *Albert W. Ketèlbey - A Master of Melody*, Basil Hogarth said of his music for the silent screen, "His orchestral music seems literally to speak, and there is no scene or situation in any picture which cannot be fitted by his extraordinarily expressive melodies", and interestingly, in commenting on the music of Ketèlbey in general, Hogarth goes on to say, "One of his most captivating charms is undoubtedly his wonderful grasp of orchestration."

Perhaps due to his success in the lighter music vein, he received little or no encouragement in his serious music aspirations, but in determination, serious pieces still flowed from his pen including the orchestral *Suite de Ballet* which was first performed at the Queen's Hall in April 1913, and the beautiful piano pieces *Berceuse, Rapsodie sérieuse, A Dream Picture* and

I see it now, the village old,
It lies enveil'd, in sunlight's gold,
The dreams of youth all come and go,
I sometimes wonder if you know!
'Twas bitter fate that led us on,
I should have known 'twas all in vain!
My heart has suffer'd sweetest pain,
But I'd live it all again!

Refrain:
Tho' 'tis far away I roam,
I can see the lights of home,
I can hear your voice so tender,
As to me it calls anew;
Tho' I know the fault was mine,
And my soul will e'er repine,
I must wander in a far land,
While my heart still clings to you!

There comes to me at twilight's hour,
A vision fair of "Lover's Bower",
I see your face in beauty wreath'd,
I hear once more the love you breath'd,
The vow we spoke with falt'ring voice
Came from the lips but not the heart!
When honour call'd and tears would start,
We still were one, - tho' doom'd to part!

Refrain:
Tho' 'tis far away I roam,
I can see the lights of home,
I can hear your voice so tender,
As to me it calls anew;
Tho' I know the fault was mine,
And my soul will e'er repine,
I must wander in a far land,
While my heart still clings to you!

Pastorale. By 1914 he had moved with Charlotte to North London, and the leafy suburbs of St. John's Wood, to a very pleasant semi-detached house at 57 Springfield Road[13], and this same year saw the publication of his story song *Keep your Toys, Laddie Boy!*

Hammond & Co. continued to publish most of his serious and other lighter compositions, but he did also begin to use other publishers such as Novello & Co. and Ascherberg, Hopwood and Crew. His ultimate aim was to persuade the larger and more famous publishing companies to publish his more serious compositions. These had the printing facilities to produce eye catching full colour pictorial and ornate covers, a valuable and augmentable marketing tool earnestly sought after at the time. In May 1915, however, it was his friend Joseph Larway, the owner of a relatively small publishing business, whom he used to publish what was to become one of the most popular pieces of British light music entitled, *In a Monastery Garden*, what Ketèlbey called a "Characteristic Intermezzo", with a beautiful full colour print of an appropriate monastery painting from the artist Aveline on its cover (see plate 25).

---

[13] Thought to be due to its close proximity to Marylebone Station, this property was destroyed by German bombers in the Second World War. A pair of modern semi-detached houses now occupy the site.

CHAPTER 5

.........INTO A MONASTERY GARDEN

.........Music is in the air, all you have to do is reach out
and take out of it what you need.

Sir Edward Elgar.

*I*n a Monastery Garden remains today as his most famous piece known all over the world, and for this reason I have devoted this chapter to the composition, which many still regard as an immortal work. In questioning the origin of the work, three possible answers came to light:-

> (1) That due to a significant lack of encouragement in pursuing his desired serious role, in response to the apparent butt of his detractors, he merely turned the slow movement of an unpublished String Quartet into the work.

> (2) That whilst driving his car from Scarborough to Bridlington he came upon an old monastery, and the calm and serenity of the place provided the idea.

> (3) The third answer goes back five years from the 1915 publication date, and whilst this provides a small story in itself, it is I believe the truth of its origin:-

Although the original idea came as in (2) above (which Ketèlbey referred to as his "first inspiration") it was not until later in 1910 that this first inspiration was re-kindled into a musical work. This happened when his friend Joseph Larway (see plate 29), who was a music publisher with offices at 14 Wells Street, off Oxford Street, London W1, invited Ketèlbey to join him on a visit to the Franciscan Friary at Chilworth, near Guildford, Surrey, to see his brother Edgar Larway (see plate 28), who had entered the Friary the previous year in September 1909 as a 21 year old novice friar. The two visitors were given a guided tour of the Friary and grounds at Chilworth, which had been built at the end of the nineteenth century, but deliberately according to medieval pattern (see plates 26 & 27). Feeling deeply moved by the quiet and solitude of the place, according to Edgar, whilst they were walking in the woods of the Friary (see plate 30), Ketèlbey turned to his friend Joseph and said, "I've got an idea......" There followed in the same year 1910 a piano composition of *In a Monastery Garden*, however, nothing was immediately published as Joseph Larway was not convinced that it would sell, and so the composer simply put it to one side.

Some two years later, in 1912, a clarinet player in the Columbia Orchestra, who spent summer seasons conducting his own orchestra at Bridlington under the pseudonym Enrico Scoma, asked Ketèlbey, his friend and impresario at Columbia, if he would write a romantic piece that his orchestra would enjoy playing at these seaside concerts. The composer thus transcribed the piano version and presented him in manuscript form an orchestral arrangement of *In a Monastery Garden*.

For two seasons Scoma included it in his concerts, and from the start it was immensely successful, with the conductor being increasingly inundated with requests for it to be played. The meticulous man that he usually was, Ketèlbey then did something uncharacteristically remiss; when although the work was yet unpublished, out of the normal sequence of events, in May 1914 on the Regal record label, he made what could have been a 'pilot' recording of it from the simple orchestral manuscript. Back at the third season of concerts at Bridlington, Scoma continued to include it in his programmes, and so popular was it that he was continuously pestered by many in his audiences, wanting to buy sheet music of the work, to the point where he was led to 'plead' with Ketèlbey to publish it.

There now arrives a little confusion to the story:-

(a)   One report states that Ketèlbey himself went back to his
        friend Larway who now agreed to publish it.

(b)   Still bearing his lofty musical ambitions however, another
        report tells of his initial reluctance to publish, and that only after
        several publishers who had come to know of the piece persistently
        asked to be allowed to issue it, did he relent.

(c)   Yet another report speaks of Ketèlbey seeing potential in the piece,
        and of his business acumen - in not allowing certain publishers the
        work because they would not meet his terms, which he eventually
        agreed with J.H. Larway.

Which ever be true, he did allow his friend Larway to publish, first the definitive piano version in April 1915, and the fuller and completed definitive orchestral version in May 1915. The latter was recorded on the Columbia label in September 1915 by the composer himself conducting the Court Symphony Orchestra, the resulting record of which incorporated on the other side the beautiful *Destiny Waltz*, by Sydney Baynes (1879 - 1938).

The above details can be substantiated by the fact that the original manuscript of the piano version (see plate 32) bears the words "Dedicated to my friend Signor Enrico Scoma", and that the same original manuscript is now in the possession of the Franciscan Brotherhood Archive, where it is proudly kept in safe custody at their Franciscan Provincial Curia in East London (see plate 31). This had been presented to them by Father Edgar Larway at his Golden Jubilee of Priesthood Celebration at the Friary, South Ascot, Berkshire, on 27th April 1967. He had cherished this manuscript for over 50 years since being presented with it by the composer shortly after it was published.

It is interesting to note that later in September 1921 Ketèlbey directed a recording on the Regal label of a waltz entitled *The Love Bird* composed by none other than Signor Enrico Scoma. Maybe this was partly done as a thank you gesture, for the role Scoma had played in the success of *In a Monastery Garden*, for regardless of the mist which seems to hang over its genesis and the fact that some believe it was paired on record with the famous *Destiny Waltz*, to add impetus to its launch, from the outset it was a huge success. With year on year sales it was truly the 'hit' of the time, and within no time at all had sold hundreds of thousands of copies of sheet music of the piano version alone, even outselling the previous piano hit in the form of *In the Shadows* by Hermann Finck (1872 - 1939). As words were set to *The Phantom Melody* to make it a song, so likewise Ketèlbey later added his own words to *In a Monastery Garden* to also make it a song, which was to further enhance its success. *In a Monastery Garden*, in its various musical forms was to become a favourite of millions - besides King George V and Queen Mary. Injured soldiers battered by war and returned home to military hospitals, found in it great comfort and solace and were therefore constantly asking for it to be played. So it was that the piece could be heard being played on the pianos of the front parlour rooms of the land; by brass and military bands, orchestras and palm court trios in parks, town halls, hotels and on seaside piers of the land, and indeed, in time, the world, and it is said that it was so liked by King George V, that quite often he had it played on the East Terrace of Windsor Castle during his evening meal. Such was the King's admiration for the piece that Sir Vivian Dunn remembered his father, William J. Dunn (both of these I speak of further in Chapter 9) telling him that when he was once playing in a military band at a court function, several members of the Royal family, who did not often take any interest in what was played, came up to the band and asked for *In a Monastery Garden* to be played.

In once writing of the success of the piece, Harry C. Burgess[14] recalled the year 1915 when as a member of Alick Maclean's Orchestra at the Spa, Scarborough, most members of the orchestra, who were recruited from various symphony orchestras in the country, tended to "pooh-pooh" this sort of composition, but that audiences seemed to acclaim it so enthusiastically that it appeared several times in their programmes. He further recalled the year 1920, when, having a few months previously returned to England after service overseas as Bandmaster of 2/5 Durham Light Infantry during the Great War, he was taking a holiday in Weston-super-Mare. Whilst here a committee responsible for entertainment asked him if he would form an orchestra, and in deciding to take up the challenge enlisted several of his Durham Light Infantry players. His "Cove" orchestra, which later became the Weston-super-Mare Municipal Orchestra, played regularly at the Rozel Bandstand in Madeira Cove, and at concerts here he said that requests to play *In a Monastery Garden* (what he called the "little novelty") were so numerous that he had to ration its performance or "risk the danger of his players becoming confirmed monks!" At this time there was also a very witty deck chair attendant who worked in Madeira Cove, who was regularly asked, "Will you ask the orchestra to play *In a Monastery Garden* please?" to which his stock answer became "Why? They're not that bad!"

Ketèlbey was very much of the mind that it was highly necessary for him to 'feel' what he wrote, and to have 'the right kind of inspiration'. In later commenting on the success of *In a Monastery Garden*, he said that to get into a suitable frame of mind whilst writing it, he had during that time of composition become an imaginary monk, and in publishing the work, he set a synopsis at the heading of the music as his own preamble, as follows:-

> "The first theme represents a poet's reverie in the quietude of the monastery garden amidst beatific surroundings - the calm serene atmosphere - the leafy trees and the singing birds. The second theme in the minor, expresses the more "personal" note of sadness, of appeal and contrition.
> Presently the monks are heard chanting the "Kyrie Eleison" (which should be sung by the orchestra) with the organ playing and the chapel-bell ringing. The first theme is now heard in a quieter manner as if it had become more ethereal and distant; the singing of the monks is again heard - it becomes louder and more insistent, bringing the piece to a conclusion in a glow of exultation."

---

14 H.C. Burgess was to become a close friend of Ketèlbey. Famous as the man who gave birth to the Weston-super-Mare Municipal Orchestra, he was later also conductor of several other orchestras, and notably the BBC Midland Light Orchestra. He also composed several light orchestral pieces.

He continued to employ this practice on several of his successful compositions which were to follow, and this led to a lot of his music quite often being referred to as "Programme Music", simply meaning music which tells a story or seeks to depict a scene, as evidenced in the classical repertoire by what are generally termed tone poems. A perfect example here is *In the Steppes of Central Asia* by Alexander Borodin (1833 - 1887) which he dedicated to Franz Liszt (1811 - 1886) who was a prolific composer of tone poems. Just as father George was a brilliant artist in painting and etching pictures, so upon writing *In a Monastery Garden* it appeared as if Albert had found his own artistic niche in painting pictures - but of the musical kind. By using the simple "In" prefix, which almost became one of his trade marks, he created several of his popular picture compositions, which were to follow, e.g. *In the Moonlight, In a Persian Market*, etc.

In the 1920s and 1930s, *In a Monastery Garden* was to become a popular request of brides - asking for it to be played in church at their weddings - mainly during the signing of the register. At one such church, St. Gabriel's in Cricklewood, London, the Vicar was a certain Mr. V. Bulman, and according to a local man, Christopher Sprigge, the Vicar was regarded by many as a 'bit of a wit', of whom Mr. Sprigge also said, "In the local press, Bulman was accustomed to "bellyache" about many different matters!" On one such occasion he apparently wrote an article about what he called the "Banal" music which brides were apt to request at his church, at the close of which he said:-

> "To crown it all on one occasion a certain bride requested that *In a Monastery Garden* should be played at her wedding, but at such a time of her life surely no bride in her senses should want to be in any Monastery garden!!"

CHAPTER 6

KETÈLBEY'S DECADE - PART ONE

THE FAME INTENSIFIES

........Thank you for the music, the songs I'm singing, thanks for all the joy they're bringing ....

Abba.

In 1915 Ketèlbey had had published *Silver Cloud - Intermezzo*, and also his *Tangled Tunes* (Potpourri) which was an arrangement of no less than 106 snippets of light and classical music by other composers, neatly dove-tailed together so as to create a continuous orchestral work. These types of arrangements were to become very popular with audiences, and were also devised by several other composers who sometimes called them a "musical switch". In his *Tangled Tunes* Ketèlbey uses a host of compositions ranging from *Three Blind Mice, Hearts of Oak, Charlie is My Darling* and *No Place Like Home* to *The Flying Dutchman Overture, William Tell Overture, The Blue Danube Waltz* and the *National Anthem* (see plate 33).

It was the popularity of *The Phantom Melody* and particularly *In a Monastery Garden*, however, which was to be the catalyst in setting him on the road to success, and combined with his experience, the success of these two pieces must have had much influence upon André Charlot bringing Ketèlbey's name fully into the spotlight in the world of variety theatre, when in 1916 he appointed Ketèlbey as Musical Director for his Revue - *Samples!* staged at the Vaudeville Theatre, on the Strand. André Charlot (1882 - 1956) was a French theatrical impresario, famous for his revues in the London theatre world in the first part of the last century, and whose influence helped to give several stars their first opportunity in the world of show business, including Noel Coward (1899 - 1973), Anna Neagle (1904 - 1986) and Gertrude Lawrence (1898 - 1952).

This opening with Charlot was to pave the way for Ketèlbey to be appointed as Musical Director for shows and pantomimes, etc. at other West

End theatres for which he would also write several songs and musical arrangements; these included, the Adelphi, the Garrick, the Shaftesbury and Drury Lane. For Charlot he was also to work at the Playhouse, St. Martin's, the Prince of Wales and the Prince's Comedy theatres, but it was the Vaudeville with which he was to have most association with these famous revues. Here, following the success of *Samples!* he was to continue in his role for several more Charlot revues. In 1916 *Some* (more samples) and *Ye Gods*; in 1917 *Cheep*; in 1918 *Tabs*, *Flora* and *The Officer's Mess*; and in 1920 *Just Fancy*. In these he quite often worked with the famous music hall singer and actress Gertie Millar, besides also working with Beatrice Lillie and even Gertrude Lawrence when she was an "unknown" in her teenage years.

The dapper little man as he was, with rimless spectacles and wavy hair parted down the middle, meant that he was easily distinguishable in these West End theatres where he worked, and where he became a popular figure with audiences. Likewise he was popular with artists and those musicians who worked under him here, and much respected for his competence and his ability to orchestrate. As one such musician once commented "You used to see him sprinkling the notes on the parts in the interval. He had it all in his head", and as another commented, in referring to his ability at making orchestral arrangements with extraordinary rapidity, "He would sit down and write out the parts and talk to you at the same time, quick as anything!" In 1975, Betty Knight recalled how at the age of ten she appeared regularly as "Betty" in *Some* in 1916, and how every night when Ketèlbey came up from the orchestra pit at the interval, he never failed to smile and speak a cheerful word to her in Italian, knowing that she spoke that language. "This kindness", she said, "I always remember as a lovely thing and clearly showed his warm-hearted nature".

In later life Ketèlbey spoke fondly and with much affection of these revues, and indeed of all of those times between 1895 to 1921 when he was actively associated with the theatre world, and his life may have been absorbed more in that sphere were it not for his deeper involvement with Columbia, and the success in composition which was to be his.

In 1918 he became a member of the Performing Right Society, which was a membership body set up in 1914 to collect income for the public performance of the works of its composer members. This was a very wise move when bearing in mind how popular his music had become, and even more so when one bears in mind that his composition of those popular light descriptive pieces for which he was to become famous, had barely begun. The following year saw the publication of one such piece, the wonderfully romantic *In the Moonlight*. As no other has painted a better musical picture of sunrise than Edvard Grieg in his *Morning*; of evening than Edward Elgar in his *Chanson de Nuit* or of a storm at sea than Nicolai Rimsky-Korsakov in his *Scheherazade*; so no one has, to my mind, painted a better musical picture of two lovers promenading arm in arm under the moon, than Ketèlbey in this piece which to me oozes 'incurable romanticism' and which his publisher Bosworth referred to as "A work of striking beauty". This was just the precursor to the decade to follow which was to be Ketèlbey's own for inspiration, fame and fortune.

It was during this time that his famous concert tours were to begin, culminating in popularity in the years of the 1930s to the point where he was called upon to conduct and perform at literally hundreds of concerts of his works all over the land, besides many on the Continent, and as early as 1919 George Cathie, the conductor of the Buxton Pavilion Gardens Orchestra, invited him to conduct that orchestra in a performance of his musical joke composition *Mind the Slide!*, written in 1915. Yes, the 1920s was to be truly "his season" from which flowed most of those successful light music compositions for which he is remembered today, and at which time other popular conductors of provincial municipal orchestras which had come into their own by now, seized hold of to include in their programmes at seaside and town hall concerts, etc. Included amongst these were Sir Dan Godfrey (Bournemouth), Henry Lyell-Tayler (Brighton and later Durban), George Bainbridge Robinson (Margate), Basil Cameron (Harrogate and Hastings), James Eldridge-Newman (Weymouth), George Cathie (North Pier, Blackpool and Buxton), Jan Hurst (South Pier - Blackpool and Bath) and Harry C. Burgess (Weston-super-Mare); most of whom were to become close friends of Ketèlbey.

In 1920 his evergreen 'gavotte' entitled *Wedgwood Blue*, was published which one commentator referred to as "Representing the composer at his daintiest", and his success in this decade was perhaps substantiated in the fact that in October 1929, in the music journal *Performing Right Gazette*, on the basis of income he was to be quoted as "Britain's greatest living composer". By this time sales of sheet music of the piano version of *In a Monastery Garden* had exceeded one million copies, and as William Neve commented in his unpublished article - "The man who sold a Million 'Monasteries'", "These were pre-pop days, but had there been charts his world famous descriptive piece would have topped them". Not all of the critics, however, were to be so favourably disposed to Mr. Ketèlbey and his music - in fact far from it, as we shall see later.

His previous and now continuing success was in no short measure due to the remarkable versatility of the man and his incredible ability to adapt himself to a wide range of exigencies within the spectrum of musical activities in which he worked, ranging from cinema and theatre to recording studio and concert performance; besides musical editing, examining and other related work, which he also undertook. There is no doubt that Bosworth & Co. the international company who became his main publishers in 1919 also played a significant part in this success. With their excellent printing facilities, high profile advertising philosophy and organisational skills he was able to entrust the publication of his compositions to their professionalism. Bosworth's were founded in 1889 in Leipzig, Germany by Arthur Edwin Bosworth, and their London Office in Heddon Street was opened in 1891. Ketèlbey was to become a close friend of Arthur Bosworth and his two sons Lawrence Owen and Arthur Ferdinand who became partners in the business, and from time to time he also did some musical editing work for them.

Bosworth's encouraged him to arrange his compositions for both piano and orchestra, the latter becoming the most popular way people enjoyed listening to light music. As Ketèlbey's success and busy schedule grew, although well able to do so himself, professional transcribers were brought in to make arrangements of his popular pieces for organ, violin and piano and other instrumental duets and music ensembles, including military and brass band. In essence Bosworth's simply exploited the potential of Ketèlbey's compositions to the full, which must have gone some way to helping him reach the pinnacle of success.

His brilliance in orchestration (which experts say was achieved through his practical understanding of so many musical instruments) brought us his *Intermezzo-Scene - In a Persian Market* (see plate 35), with its diversity of sometimes amusing, sometimes pensive tunes, the amazing origins of which he once recalled to Wilfred Dorrington, his Isle of Wight chauffeur as follows:-

> A producer of a pantomime in London asked Ketèlbey if he could write a short piece of descriptive music depicting an eastern scene with a camel train, lasting for four minutes. The composer set to this and presented the music to the producer, who upon playing discovered that at six minute duration it ran for too long for the scene in question. He duly contacted the composer again and asked him if he could shorten it, but Ketèlbey refused. In his dilemma the producer asked him "What am I supposed to do", to which Ketèlbey replied "Put in some more bloody camels!" - and apparently that was what was done.

Although said in jest Ketèlbey's suggestion was perhaps an ungrateful response to the man who instigated the piece, for in truth it was to become a phenomenal success for the composer, some saying even more so than *In a Monastery Garden*. A light musical piece of the Orient, it's various parts were clearly defined in Ketèlbey's own synopsis ..... "The camel drivers gradually approach the market; the cries of beggars for "Back-sheesh" are heard amid the bustle. The beautiful princess enters carried by her servants, (she is represented by a languorous theme, given at first in clarinet and cello, then repeated by full orchestra) - she stays to watch the jugglers and snake-charmer. The Caliph now passes through the market and interrupts the entertainment, the beggars are heard again, the princess prepares to depart and the caravan resumes its journey; the themes of the princess and the camel-drivers are heard faintly in the distance and the market-place becomes deserted".

It was simply 'a natural', played in its entirety or in part, in depicting eastern and oriental scenes on the silent movie screen and in stage productions. This, together with the fact that millions simply liked to hear it for its own sake as a piece of light hearted music, meant that it came to be played literally all over the world. It has been said, that with the exception of the national anthem, and at the height of silent movies, it was probably played more frequently than any other composition in the history of British music. How it fared in Russia I do not know, though amazingly (and presumably with this world famous piece in mind) a Soviet spokesman once declared "Ketèlbey's alluring exoticism is a piece of cleverly masked Imperial Propaganda!"

In commenting on the success of this piece H.C. Burgess conductor of the Weston-super-Mare Municipal Orchestra once said, "Oh so many requests came for this number that it became a nuisance to a conductor who wished to play more serious music". Apropos it led to our witty deckchair attendant, previously referred to in Chapter 5, when also now asked "Will you ask the orchestra to play *In a Persian Market* please", to respond in his jesting style, "Yes, but who's going to pay the fare?"

In fact so many were the number of recordings of the piece in the 1920s in various instrumental modes, that one critic writing in *The Gramophone* in March 1928, and commenting on yet "another" recording said, "I have been encouraged to think and hope during the last few months that even the recording companies had unanimously agreed that this effusion had been recorded ad nauseam". Interestingly one of the first military bands to record the piece was the Birmingham Police Band, and even today the BBC holds close on 100 different recordings of *In a Persian Market* in its record library!

The so called 'Sand Dance' from *In a Persian Market* (which is actually the camel driver's theme from the piece) was to become very popular with comedy acts, and especially the revered British comedy trio of "Wilson, Keppel and Betty", whose own famous and very amusing 'Sand Dance' was always the hallmark of their variety act.

The year 1921 saw the publication of *Evening Calm - Nocturne*; the beautiful *Gallantry - Intermezzo Romance*, in which is demonstrated his brilliance in counterpoint; and *A Desert Romance - Descriptive Sketch*, which he dedicated to his friend Henry Lyell-Tayler, the conductor of the Brighton Municipal Orchestra. In the same year his intermezzo of English villages set amongst country fields and meadows in the lovely *Bells across the Meadows* was published by Keith Prowse & Co. Ltd., with a delightful full colour print on the cover by the artist W. George, depicting a young maiden in contemplative mood looking out over a village and the English countryside (see plate 39). It is quite incredible to think that the client who commissioned a piece of music actually rejected this one as having no future. Ketèlbey who loved the warm tones of tubular bells had, however, set about composing the piece with much enthusiasm and, not believing for a minute that it had no future, managed to persuade Sir Dan Godfrey to include it in one of his concerts with the Bournemouth Municipal Orchestra, and from that moment on it was a huge success.

Although Ketèlbey made no written mention of it, I was told by Marie Haddleton of Great Barr, Birmingham, that she believed his inspiration for this piece went back to his childhood memories of the peeling bells of Aston Parish Church - the Church of St. Peter and St. Paul, built in the 15th century and located in Witton Lane, Aston. During the early part of last century Marie's grandmother lived at Serpentine Road, Aston Manor, and her neighbours here were a family by the name of Willmore, who like the Ketelbeys had worked for many years in the Birmingham Jewellery Quarter, and it was from this family source that Marie's grandmother had been told of this early inspiration behind the famous piece. The area where this church still stands bears little resemblance today in appearance to as it was in the 1870s and 1880s, when what is today Nelson, Jardine and Endicott Roads and Aston Villa's football ground complex, was then known as Aston Lower Grounds.

In its day this was one of the most popular places for recreation and sports events in the Midlands, and some of the main features incorporated within the site were a sports meadow - sometimes called 'The Magnificent Meadow', ornamental gardens, two bowling greens, a large fish pond called Dovehouse Pool (located where Aston Villa's pitch is today) and the Great Hall where concerts, theatrical and music hall productions, etc. were performed.

Other features included a roller skating rink, an aquarium, a tobogganing slide, a band stand and even a switchback railway. On the sports meadow were played cricket and football matches, and athletics and cycling events were held here regularly, and various prominent teams and personalities of the day often participated in these. As a place of recreation where people could watch sport, and where families could walk and picnic, listen to the band and watch regular firework displays, it was within walking distance of Albert's early homes in Aston Manor, and it is indeed highly likely that George and Sarah would have taken their children for outings here - and when so doing young Albert would indeed have heard the bells of the church peeling over the meadow!

As popular as the piece became, some time later the BBC banned it from being broadcast. This happened during the Second World War, when following a performance of it on *Forces Favourites* on the night of Monday 20th August 1941, there was the following day a stern reprimand issued by the Controller of Programmes at the BBC. This concerned the possible repercussions of playing peeling bells over the air waves, as quite easily being interpreted by the listening public as the signal of a "Warning of Invasion" - which the said Controller had previously, and quite clearly, brought to the attention of his subordinates by official memorandum. Therefore, after learning of *Bells across the Meadows* being broadcast (with its quite distinctive peeling of bells at beginning and end) he was 'far from amused' and following his reprimand in being held responsible for the playing of *Bells across the Meadows*, Mr. Leslie A. Perowne issued the following edict to all concerned parties at the BBC, regardless of how popular the piece was;-

BELLS ACROSS THE MEADOWS. A.W. KETÈLBEY.
PROHIBITION

LAP/AMH   21st August 1941
   Will you please note that this composition contains
unaccompanied church bells, which as you know, should
not be broadcast on any account. Will you please therefore
mark the index card in the Gramophone Library "N.T.B.B"
for the duration of the war.
(N.T.B.B. = Not to be broadcast).

In fact so popular was it that within weeks of being published in 1921, it seemed it was being played almost endlessly all over the land, and Sir Dan Godfrey told the story of one gentleman, who having just wined and dined in Bournemouth (and having taken his 'liquid refreshment' portion to some excess) when upon leaving the restaurant and hearing the *Bells across the Meadows* coming from a performance in the Winter Gardens, was heard to exclaim "1812 again......I'm sick of that damn thing!!"

Paradoxically if the gods of innovation had been on Ketèlbey's side with regard to the timing of the development and expansion of the gramophone record as a medium for listening to his music, then regardless of the "Bells-Hiccup" which was to befall him later, the same gods must have played a similar part with radio, when in 1922 the BBC began broadcasting its regular service. Through the great influence of Sir John Reith, once "red tape" and initial restrictive regulations concerning the broadcasting of music had been eradicated, music was to occupy a large part of its programmes, and within just four years with some two million radio licences held, there were estimated to be several million listeners to the new medium - the timing of which was just perfect for Mr. Ketèlbey and his popular compositions.

Regarding these compositions, there had by now appeared on the scene an individual who was working for Ketèlbey and whose job almost amounted to being "Compositions Security Officer", and his name was Tommy Kottaun. He was a cornet player who had both played regularly under Ketèlbey and acted as orchestral librarian when required, but who unfortunately did not enjoy the best of health, and so was often prevented from playing. He had much admiration for Mr. K., and likewise Ketèlbey had much regard for him, seeing him as a willing hand in whom he could trust, and to try and help Tommy in his situation, he took him on as a kind of agent. As there is piracy today in the realms of popular compact discs and videos etc., where crooks try to pass off imitations for the genuine article, so was often the case with popular sheet music in Ketèlbey's day. The way to combat this was for the composer actually to sign the cover of the sheet music as proof of its authenticity. The problem here of course was the sheer volume of those popular compositions, *In a Monastery Garden* being a perfect example, whereby the solution was for the composer to have cut a perfect replica of his signature as a rubber stamp, which would then be inked and stamped on the cover by the publisher before being sent out to retail and other outlets. As his "agent", Ketèlbey gave Tommy Kottaun the job of doing this stamping job, instead of the publishers. He actually became known as Ketèlbey's "checker" because whilst he was stamping he would keep an accurate record of the number of sheets processed, so that his shrewd boss could keep tabs on the exact volume of sales of each of his compositions! So Tommy would do his rounds of the publishers with the famous rubber stamp, and Margaret Sharpe (née Ashdown) once a director of the publishers Edwin Ashdown Ltd. (who in 1929 incorporated the publishing house J.H. Larway within their business) once recalled that as a young girl she remembered Tommy as a great character, doing his "checking and stamping", when he could process copies of *In a Monastery Garden* at the incredible rate of 5,000 per hour - and continue talking at the same time!

With his propensity to compose now increasing, in 1923 there came *In a Chinese Temple Garden - Oriental Fantasy* (see plate 41), again confirming his incredible pictorial imagination, which several people have said he inherited from his artist father. So meticulous was Ketèlbey to get the atmosphere and pictures correct in this work of the Orient, that he visited the British Museum to do his homework on Chinese music and culture. Thus in his finished work the music depicting a street fight in Shanghai between Chinese coolies is founded on the actual Chinese scale, and even the words given to the priests melody are the actual Chinese words of the Canton dialect phonetically spelt.

In 1924 his *Suite romantique* was published, which he dedicated to his friend Sir Dan Godfrey the conductor of the Bournemouth Municipal Orchestra. This orchestra gave the first performance of the definitive work under the baton of the composer during a Bournemouth Musical Festival on 10th April 1924. Very "Elgarian" in style and with high emotional content in its first movement *Romance*, this work is most definitely Ketèlbey in serious mood, the other two movements being *Scherzo* and *Valse dramatique*. Interestingly, it would appear that this suite (or an earlier version) had in fact already been given a performance at the Trinity College of Music Jubilee Concert on 14th June 1922 at the Queen's Hall, when Ketèlbey conducted the work which he then called simply his *Romantic Suite*, and which upon hearing a celebrated London critic said, "The orchestration is delicious". Also in 1924 were published the *Chal Romano Overture*, sometimes called *Gipsy Lad* in which he depicts the atmosphere of Romany life, the song *Will you forgive?* and the evergreen and very moving *Sanctuary of the Heart* - which he called a *Meditation Religieuse* - and which simple yet beautiful melody he said was inspired by the beauty and deep spirituality of the wife of his friend George Bainbridge Robinson, the conductor of the Margate Municipal Orchestra, and Boosey's Concert Orchestra during the season of Ballad Concerts held at the Royal Albert Hall. Ketèlbey once said, "There are four indispensable requirements of successful light music: sincerity, emotional impulse, vigour of rhythm and good craftsmanship" - traits which to my mind exude from *Sanctuary of the Heart*, perhaps his most moving composition.

Intermingled with these and other light pieces, such as another Potpourri *A Musical Jig-saw*, he still published 'serious' piano music, several of which

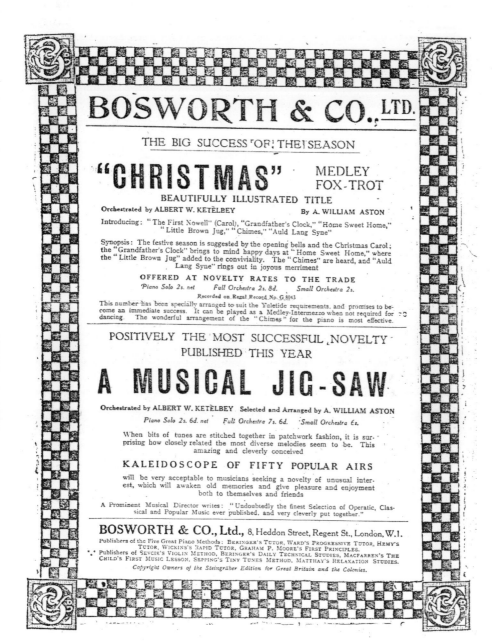

One of Bosworth & Co's full page advertisements.
Musical Opinion & Music Trade Review - December 1923.
"Reproduced by permission of Bosworth & Company Ltd., 8/9 Frith Street, London."

pieces I have grown to love. These include *Reflections* (1921), *Sunset Glow* (1921) in which can be clearly heard the sound of his favourite tubular bells, *The Shadow of Dreams* (1922), *Golden Autumn* (1923) and *Love's Devotion* (1924). Whether the American composer and pianist David Dreyer heard the penultimate composition before he published in 1927 his song *Me and My Shadow*, made famous by Al Jolson, I know not, but the opening bars of the song do bear a remarkable resemblance to the opening bars of Ketèlbey's *Golden Autumn*. In publishing *A Musical Jig-saw* previously referred to he used a new pseudonym in listing the credits as "Selected and Arranged by A. William Aston, Orchestrated by Albert W. Ketèlbey". (Aston was of course both his mother's maiden name and the place of his birth). In the winter of the same year (1923) was also published a festive Potpourri in the form of a Medley Fox-Trot entitled *Christmas* and here again the credits are listed as "By A. William Aston, Orchestrated by Albert W. Ketèlbey.

What the public wanted, however, was more of his characteristic light music, a fact confirmed when following the performance of his compositions *Suite romantique* and *Chal Romano Overture* at the Bournemouth Festival Concerts at Easter 1924, the *Musical Opinion* of June 1924 in reporting on the concerts stated:-

> "A. W. Ketèlbey's frankly "popular" pieces, played last year, are decidedly more worthy of attention than his Suite and Overture, both on more serious lines, heard on this occasion."

In 1921 he and Lottie had moved home again, when amid much excitement, with the help of their friends George Bainbridge Robinson and his wife, they moved to the fashionable suburbs of Hampstead to live at 15 Frognal[15]. Once settled into their new home at Frognal, it was not long before Albert had installed in the basement room a full sized billiards table. In out-door pursuits he enjoyed playing golf and motoring, and was also very keen on cinematography to the point of owning a cine-camera, but when at home, besides his music and what he called his 'hobby' of playing his favourite musical instrument - the cello, his other great love was billiards. He had taken an interest in the game earlier in his life, and now with his own table and a keen eye for the game he was to become an enthusiastic and able player, and would derive immense pleasure and relaxation in assessing the angles and making his "good leaves" on the green baize, even having special spectacles made for the purpose - long before Dennis Taylor thought of the idea!

---

[15] This huge and rather grand semi-detached property, although now converted to flats, its exterior frontage, with the exception of alterations made to the entrance door, remains as it was when Ketèlbey lived there (see plate 37).

For New Year's Eve 1922 Albert and Lottie arranged a fancy dress party at their Frognal home, to which were invited Lottie's relatives and a few close friends, and which was to become an annual event at the Ketèlbey's home. For this, he asked Jack Ockenden, a long standing friend and colleague who was a violinist with the Columbia Orchestra, to arrange and lead a trio, with Jack on violin, Harold Perry on piano and another Columbia colleague on drums. The following is a reproduction of the letter which Ketèlbey sent to Ockenden in connection with this party, setting out precise instructions in his typical "cross the t's and dot the i's" style, even for such a light hearted event.

Dec.19th 1922   15 Frognal,
                                                          Hampstead, N.W.3
Dear Ockenden,

> Yours received, right-o that will be alright, - be here at 10 o'clock (not any sooner) & tell the others to come in very quietly as I don't want the guests to know anything about the band till they start playing. I will tell the maid to show you all into the billiards room & then I will come down & arrange with you what to do. I want to dress you all up in some funny clothes (alleged funny!) like a nigger band, we shall all be dressed up like a lot of guys so the men won't feel conspicuous!

Yours sincerely,

Albert W. Ketèlbey.

N.B. Come to Finchley Rd. station (Met) from Baker St. turn to left into Finchley Rd. 2nd on the Right (off Finchley Rd.)

The bank holiday scenes he was to observe on Hampstead Heath near to his new home, provided the idea for the fifth movement of his *Cockney Suite* published in 1924. Though proud of his Birmingham roots he enjoyed living in London and often said he was "A Brummie by birth and a Cockney by adoption" though his youngest sister Doris referred to his association with the capital in much stronger terms, when she said, "He took to London like a fish to water and sank himself in it", and according to her even more so after marrying Lottie - whose family were very much Londoners. There must have therefore been some real meaning when he once said that he "enjoyed soaking up the atmosphere of the capital", and indeed such was his constant amusement at   Cockney slang, that in good fun and typical Cockney style he often referred to his tunes as "My Chunes".

The *Cockney Suite* is his own salute to London and covers a diverse range of moods and scenes over the five movements, the fourth movement of which in later years Ketèlbey referred to as one of his finest compositions.

The movements are:-

(1) *A State Procession* march depicting the royal coach journey from Buckingham Palace to Westminster, for the State Opening of Parliament

(2) *Cockney Lover* an elaboration upon the whistling of the song "Arf a pint of mild and bitter".

(3) *At the Palais de Danse* a graceful waltz with jazz connotations.

(4) *Elegy* depicting solemn thoughts whilst passing the Cenotaph Memorial in Whitehall.

(5) *Bank Holiday 'Appy 'Ampsted* depicting Bank Holiday on Hampstead Heath, in which he humorously evokes many of the genuine sounds he heard for himself when strolling through the Heath on Bank Holiday Monday, including mouth organs, spoon and bone players, a busking cornet player, roisterers bawling the words of *Tell me the old, old story*, of fairground callers wielding football rattles before shouting "Walk up, walk up - all the fun of the fair", and even a short rendition of *There is a Tavern in the Town*, and Rosas[16] famous waltz - *Over the Waves!*

By the mid 1920s Ketèlbey's success was such that his compositions could be heard several times a day in cinemas, restaurants and tea rooms throughout the land. Indeed, live in-shop musical entertainment had become so popular by now that the Lyons Teashop chain alone were investing in excess of

---

16 Juventino Rosas (1868 - 1894).

£150,000.00 a year in it, mainly in the form of trios. He would still take up opportunities to appear as solo pianist in London and the provinces, but by now a popular conductor, the people perhaps enjoyed him more conducting orchestras and military and brass bands, at concerts of his own and others music in London, Birmingham, Manchester and many other provincial and sea-side towns and cities.

In the winter of 1926 another festive medley *A Dream of Christmas* was published, but this time under his own name, and this was advertised as being "A Novelty for Christmas and a Speciality for 'Community' Singing". A recording by the Court Symphony Orchestra and Chorus on the Columbia label was issued in December 1926, but a larger force recording embracing concert orchestra, organ, chorus, solo vocalist and narrator was to be later recorded on the same label and issued in November 1929.

CHAPTER 7

KETÈLBEY'S DECADE - PART TWO
THE GOOD TIMES

........there is nothing better for men than to be happy and do good while they live. That every man may eat and drink, and find satisfaction in all his toil - this is the gift of God.

Solomon.

$\mathcal{B}$y the middle of the decade Ketèlbey knew very well that it was his aptitude for light music which had brought him his success, and in 1925 this was confirmed when his light hearted and romantic *Suite - In a Lovers' Garden* was published. This delightful and 'typical' Ketèlbey work, with his favourite tubular bells making their entry in the second movement, was based upon tunes from songs he had previously written, and should, in my opinion, be reckoned amongst his popular works, the three movements being;-

1. *A Song of Love* (from *Under the Starlight* and *My Heart Still Clings to You*)
2. *The Golden Wedding* (from *The Old Ingle-nook* and *At Parting*)
3. *A Garden Fête* (from *Fairy Butterfly*).

Also published in the same year, and serving to confirm his light music forte, was *In a Camp of the Ancient Britons - Fantasy*, and in reminiscing about his friendly association with Ketèlbey, H. C. Burgess recalled how this piece came to be written. This happened when he invited the composer to Weston-super-Mare for the weekend of 9th and 10th August 1924, and on the Sunday evening to conduct Burgess's "Cove" Orchestra at a concert at Knightstone Pavilion on Knightstone Island, consisting entirely of Ketèlbey's compositions. Harold Hartley of Coleford, Gloucestershire remembered this weekend, when as a violinist in the "Cove" Orchestra he worked into the early hours copying by hand violin parts for Ketèlbey. He also had a vivid memory of the surprise all of the members of the orchestra felt at some of Ketèlbey's "tempos", and particularly what he called his "'show piece' *Monastery Garden*", which he said, "travelled along at about 120 beats per minute, or even faster, under his baton".

On the Sunday morning of the particular weekend, Burgess took both Albert and wife Lottie on a brief tour of some of the interesting spots in Weston, and included in the tour was a visit to the ruins of Worlebury Hillfort - British Camp - set in the woods on the hillside behind Weston, and dating back to the time of the Romans. Burgess recalled that Ketèlbey was quite impressed with the site and stayed a long time there taking in the atmosphere of the place. A little later he told Burgess that he was going to compose "a little number" to mark the occasion and suggested that he would dedicate it to him. In kind gesture, however, Burgess said it would be better if he dedicated it to a Captain Matthews, who was not only a keen archaeologist but also Editor of the *Weston Gazette*, and this would ensure the work had plenty of publicity. *In a Camp of the Ancient Britons* thus came into being in the summer of 1925 bearing the words "Dedicated to my friends at Weston, Mr. H. C. Burgess and Captain Matthews", and Ketèlbey said of the work, "My tone picture *In a Camp of the Ancient Britons* was inspired by a visit to Weston-super-Mare. When I saw the gay promenade, and in the background the old ramparts (Worlebury), carrying the mind back to the time of the Roman Legions and the Druids, I felt the vividness of the contrast, and wrote the music that, I hope, conveys the atmosphere of the old drama, gradually merging into the present-day brightness and gaiety". The work is also "typical" Ketèlbey, including again tubular bells and setting the various moods with some high emotional content, and H. C. Burgess further recalled that following its composition he gave it several performances, but that sadly it never seemed to have the same impact as some of his other compositions.

And yet underneath did there still lie some frustration in not attaining his goal as a serious composer? Could this be the reason why he took on the mantle of "knight errant" in attacking the criticism by "Schaunard" of the serious composition *A World Requiem* by his contemporary light music composer John H. Foulds (1880 - 1939). Amazingly, although he barely knew Foulds, he contended in heated, even sometimes rude, debate with "Schaunard" in a saga of correspondence in the letter pages of the *Musical Opinion* for some four months from December 1924 to March 1925, the extent of which would require a chapter of its own in this book! Neither really won the argument, which in essence was to whether the piece was a 'quality' serious work by an otherwise light composer, except that Ketèlbey did little to further his cause with the world of the critics - rather the opposite!

By the mid 1920s Lottie's brothers were progressing well within their respective furnishing businesses. Brother Louis was now also fulfilling mayoral and councillor roles on the local Islington Council, besides chairing the Islington Shopping Week Festival. It also appears that several members of the Lewis/Curzon family took an active part in Islington Chamber of Commerce, especially social events such as the annual dinner and dance, to which the Ketèlbeys were regularly invited, as illustrated in the amusing letter shown on page 67.

In early 1925 the couple moved home again, but not far this time, choosing to stay in the Hampstead area they had grown so fond of, they simply moved around the corner from 15 Frognal to a larger house at 15 Lindfield Gardens[17]. This was to become his most cherished abode, and where they were to stay for the rest of the time they were to live in London. Complete with a very spacious basement which led out to a large rear garden, Albert was easily able to transfer his billiards table to the basement of his new home. Here the annual New Year's Eve parties continued with the "Ockenden Trio", and here also there were to be regular Sunday morning social gatherings. With the exception of a handful of close family friends, all of the guests at these Sunday morning gatherings (and indeed the New Year's Eve parties) were Jewish relations of Lottie. Their friend Harry C. Burgess and his wife were invited to these functions on several occasions, but unfortunately were never able to make the journey from Weston-super-Mare. Friends who were regular attenders included Walton O'Donnell[18], and George Bainbridge Robinson and his wife and three children, who lived close by at the Ridgway, Golders Green.

Albert and Lottie loved children and as they had none of their own, it was good enough reason why their Hampstead home was always open to the nieces and nephews of Lottie's family and the children of their close friends, particularly on a Sunday morning, where they would receive every encouragement from their Uncle Albert in their favourite song or party piece. Miss Catherine Robinson (the youngest daughter of George Bainbridge Robinson) had many memories of her family's association with the Ketèlbey's. She recalled the close friendship of her father (see plate 43) with her "Uncle Albert", and how he took an interest and helped her father (originally a clarinettist) to improve a new style of clarinet mouthpiece he had designed and later patented. "Uncle Albert", she said, "was a jolly lively

---

17 This traditional but very impressive large detached property, although converted to flats in 1948, remains from the exterior as it was when Ketèlbey lived there (see plate 36).

18 Walton O'Donnell (1887 - 1939) was a composer of military and light music, though he is remembered today more for his association with military music. In 1927, having served as Musical Director of the Royal Marines for ten years, he retired to set up and direct the BBC Military Band, which by the 1930s was reckoned to be one of the finest military bands in the world.

16 Glenavon Close,
Claygate,
Surrey.   24.2.75

Dear Mr. Neve,

Even after 50 years I have a very vivid memory of Albert Ketelbey. From the age of 14 my parents would take my sister and me to the annual dinner and dance of the Islington Chamber of Commerce where we would link up with him and his party in a casual way.

To me he seemed a very small elderly gentleman - he must have been all of 41 - *[he was actually nearer 51]* very shy but very gentle. He would dance with me (or should I say shuffle round) probably, now I come to think about it, because on the first occasion at least I was one of the few females who didn't tower above him, and would enquire gently about my school pursuits and achievements.

Now my mother was besotted by Ketelbey's music and in retrospect I can only remember Monastery Garden, Persian Market and occasionally Bells across the Meadow ever being played by her either on the piano or the gramophone, so that when at the Chamber of Commerce dinner the group of musicians on the balcony would churn out the same three pieces, my sister and I would have the utmost difficulty in refraining from bursting into paroxysms of mirth.

By the age of 16 I had lost my inhibitions and any awe I may have had of our celebrity. (I was also considerably taller) and having informed him of my mother's passion for his music and mentioning our records were almost worn out with constant playing, I was emboldened to ask him if he ever got tired of constantly hearing the music he had composed. He looked me straight in the eye and said "Don't you?" And being young and cheeky I can remember saying "Well, yes a bit. But it's very pretty". to me he was a dear little man.

I am afraid I cannot help you in regard to details about the lady *[Lottie]* although I do remember she was rather a little lady, and they were reputed to be a very devoted couple. I am sure my sister and I were rather more occupied at the time in searching out the younger male talent in the congregation!

Yours sincerely,

Kay Morgan (Mrs.)

man, entertaining and full of jokes", and remembered him telling her once that when he told a lady that he played the organ with his feet - she thought he was either making fun or was an acrobat!

Catherine said that both Albert and Lottie were very kind towards her, as a crippled and shy child, but mentioned in particular the fact that her older sister Teresa and brother Jack were treated by them as if they were their own children (see plate 44).   Interestingly Catherine's favourite "Uncle" was Roger Quilter (1877 - 1953), the composer, who was also a very close friend of her parents; as too was the famous Australian composer Percy Aldridge Grainger (1882 - 1961).   Teresa was artistically inclined and was often invited to stay for a few days with them, and at one time her ability was put to good use when Lottie asked her to paint scenes on wall panels in their home, for which she was said to be well paid.   On another occasion Albert encouraged her talent when he asked her to paint the scenes for the covers of two of his compositions *Algerian Scene* (1925) and *In a Fairy Realm* (1928).   Her brother Jack (who became a medical student at Guy's Hospital) proved to be particularly good at billiards, no doubt his ability encouraged by Uncle Albert, and more often than not Jack would win the billiards contests held at the Sunday morning gatherings.

In other recollections Catherine Robinson explained in some detail the extremes of the personalities of the Ketèlbeys, where on the one hand she refers to Albert as being kind and generous; on the other she refers to both him and Lottie as being possessive and quite demanding. Both, she said, were highly strung and would take offence quickly. Both were apt to be temperamental and to row with each other, though for all this they were much liked by family and friends and renowned by all to be devoted to each other. In fact such was Lottie's devotion to Albert that she was often over-protective towards him, sometimes referring to him lovingly as "my Ket". Likewise his devotion to her meant that he cherished her companionship wherever he went, to the point where he could be purported to be "under her thumb" and lacking in freedom to go off on his own. It has to be said, however, that Lottie herself helped to paint this dominative picture in tending perhaps too often to answer for Albert during conversations, and in particular in having fitted on their motor car her own rear view mirror and hooter!! Amusingly Lottie once commented "I trust Ket's driving, but I have my own driving mirror and hooter, so that I can help him". Like many musicians of the time "her Ket" liked a powerful car, and it was perhaps with these comments of Lottie's in mind that in his wry mischievous style, he is reputed to have once said, "I like powerful cars because they are safer at level-crossings!" The car in question at this time was a dark blue Chrysler, in which he took much pride.

Other activities at these Sunday morning gatherings included tennis on the court in the rear garden and long walks on their favourite Hampstead Heath, and on some occasions Albert and Lottie would entertain about fifteen members of the family to Sunday lunch at Frascati's or the Trocadero. A favourite nephew of Albert was Louis Lewis Junior, the son of Lottie's brother Louis, and Michael Lewis the son of Louis Junior recalled cherished memories of his Great Uncle Albert, and his interesting tales, particularly of concerts he had conducted. Albert and Lottie's continuing love for the theatre is evidenced in the fact that for many years they took their great nephew Michael and his sister Cynthia and their mother Dorothy to pantomime performances at the Lyceum, and Michael could remember Sunday mornings at Uncle Albert's house, when, "While the ladies chatted in the drawing room, the gentlemen descended to the lower ground floor to play billiards on his full sized table".

The New Year's Eve parties were jovial affairs - where Albert's good sense of fun came to the fore. Each year he and Lottie would decide upon a theme and all of the guests were to attend duly attired in suitable fancy dress, and more often than not Albert would dress as the 'pantomime dame' (see plate 40). All who attended were expected to do their party piece of song or recitation, etc. and one popular monologue of the time, which all found very funny (and which still evokes laughter today) was *Albert and the Lion*, which was his brother-in-law Louis's regular spot. Although Michael Lewis was too young at the time to join these parties, he could remember his mother and father making their fancy dress costumes and struggling to learn the words of some song or recitation, and Catherine Robinson recalled how lively Aunty Lottie was when she sang her number and "gesticulated a lot".

Even for the musical content at these parties, Ketèlbey was quite precise with his instructions to his friend Ockenden, as the letter on page 71 referring to the 31st December 1931 party confirms. He would encourage the trio to enter into the fun of the party, and ask Ockenden to play dance arrangements of his popular pieces such as *In a Persian Market*, and nearly always would ask him to see if he could arrange to bring along to the party some of his favourite tubular bells for an "authentic" midnight celebration. Albert and Lottie as the hosts, truly entered into the full spirit of these extravaganzas, and at the end of the night after all the guests had marched around singing *All good pals and jolly good company*, it was always "Uncle Albert" who would remain at the centre of the fun and lead them all in the Conga!

Wed.

Dear Ockenden

Will you & the bandits be here on Saturday next at 11
o'clock. Please bring plenty of "Paul Jones" music,
they seem to like this dance very much, also The "Jolly
Good Company" piece.

With kindest regards & best wishes to you & Mrs.
Ockenden for 1932.

      Yours sincerely,

      Albert W. Ketèlbey

Albert W. Ketèlbey

Composer and Conductor

Hampstead 2066

15 LINDFIELD GARDENS,
HAMPSTEAD, N.W. 3.

Wed.

Dear McKenden

Will you & The bandits be here on Saturday next at 11 o'clock. Please bring plenty of "Paul Jones" music, they seem to like this dance very much, also the "Jolly Good Company" piece.

With kindest regards & best wishes to you & Mrs McKenden for 1932

Yours sincerely

Albert W. Ketèlbey

Jack Ockenden served Ketèlbey in his trio capacity at these parties from 1922 to 1932, but for the 1932 party he was unwell and so his son Jack Junior, then just 19 years of age, deputised for his father, and when in November 1974 William Neve visited him at his Surbiton home, he shared his and his fathers memories of their association with Mr. K, which fortunately William documented. It is the virtues of kindness and generosity, of Ketèlbey the man, which again shine through in the record of these memories.

He showed William the cut glass and silver bowl which Albert and Lottie presented to his parents when they were married in 1912, and spoke of the year when as a young man he deputised for his father, feeling rather overawed by the occasion and on his mettle. Mr. K was, however, most understanding, and he remembered being shown into the billiards room (like his father before him), being given a good meal with his colleagues, and having been put at ease by the host, thoroughly enjoying himself all evening. He spoke of Lottie as being rather petite, very pleasant and much loved by all the guests, and he also mentioned how she protected her husband from the outside world to the point where he depended upon her very much. In the early 1930s a violinist playing in a London theatre orchestra would earn approximately £6.00 per week, so when Ketèlbey paid the trio £10.00 each year for one to two hours playing, as mentioned in his letter of thanks to Ockenden for the 31st December 1930 party, and reproduced on page 75, this was good money, on top of enjoying and being very much a part of the party.

Unfortunately Jack Senior's health did not improve and he became seriously ill. This prompted Mr. K to write to his son in kindly and concerned terms regarding practicalities, making particular mention of the hard times through which everyone was going during this period of the depression. Sadly when his father died later in 1933, again Mr. K put pen to paper, and as Jack Junior said, sent a personal letter of condolence to his mother couched in terms of straight forward sympathy, and delicately worded in his bold unfaltering hand. Indeed the passing of Jack Ockenden Senior may well have ended an era of New Year's Eve merrymaking at the Ketèlbey home, for as far as is known no such parties took place there after his death.

The strange trait in the midst of all of this socialising, grand life style and generosity, was the apparent exclusion of his own family in Birmingham, with whom Albert now appeared to have little or no contact, although some form of contact did continue between himself and his younger academic sister Doris. This area remains a very grey one, for although brother

Harold, who was now working out his own musical career in South Africa, did visit Albert and Lottie with his family when he made a return visit to England in 1927, as far as is known, neither his parents or sisters and their families were ever invited for New Year's Eve or any social weekend. Logical reasons which would immediately come to mind here, would be those of distance, time and travel and relative costs, and yet when one takes into account the facts of how much his parents had encouraged him and sacrificed, in order to give him his musical start in life, and with his older sisters Florence and Edith being of lower-middle or working class, surely it would not have been unnatural for the millionaire son and brother to occasionally treat all to the train fare and accommodation, in order that they could join in the happiness and fun of his success?

Father George had strong prejudices against actresses, and like many people of his background, did he also have similar prejudices against Jews? With Lottie also being of German stock, was all of this too much to bear in a daughter-in-law whose domineering personality matched and rivalled his own? Some have said that George never truly forgave his oldest son for abandoning, or purporting to abandon, his career in serious music, and George may well have seen Lottie as being very much a part of Albert's digression. All of this would have no doubt caused some friction for the whole family, and did Albert therefore assume that this rift with his father extended to the rest of his family in Birmingham, which in turn precluded them all? When once having told his sister Doris of the success of his concerts abroad, he went on to say "I hope I have not disgraced our family name", and this strange statement may be significant in the context of his relation-ship with his father and family in Birmingham. Had he found an aspect of happiness in the Siegenberg family, which as a child he had not experienced in his own, whereby their affection towards him meant that he simply immersed himself with them - without any other thought? Or could their exclusion have been part of Lottie's over protection of Albert - even from his own family, or even her own unchallenged selfishness, when as one who knew her once said, that under her influence "He seemingly had only her friends"? All of this is of course purely speculative, and the true answer could be a combination of all of these, or indeed some other reason(s), but this sad family aspect - completely out of Albert's normal character - has dumbfounded several people, not least surviving family members in Birmingham. One thing however, which remained constant throughout Albert's life - and which maybe confuses this matter even further - was the underlying love and respect he always had for his father, whereby he always

Jan 5/31

My Dear Ockenden

I enclose cheque for £10 for the Trio, with thanks for the nice way you all stayed on & helped the show along. I trust the amount of cheque will be satisfactory. With kind regards & best wishes.

Yours sincerely,

Albert W. Ketèlbey

"*Probably no-one to-day has more completely the flair for light popular music than Mr. Ketèlbey.*"
—Daily Telegraph.

Composer of the following popular world-successes:

"In a Monastery Garden"
"In a Persian Market"
"Sanctuary of the Heart"
"Bells across the Meadows"
"In a Chinese Temple-Garden"
etc., etc.

Albert W. Ketèlbey

Composer and Conductor

Hampstead 2026

15 LINDFIELD GARDENS,
HAMPSTEAD, N.W. 3.

Jan 5/31

My dear Ockenden

I enclose cheque for £10 for the Trio, with thanks for the nice way you all stayed on & helped the show along. I trust the amount of cheque will be satisfactory. With kind regards & best wishes

Yours sincerely

Albert W. Ketèlbey

to the end of his life kept a picture of his father hung in his study. I am of
the firm belief that the breach of his relationship with his father left a deep
and lasting scar on his heart. Whilst he never spoke of such, I am convinced
that there is in much of his music an undertone "of a yearning" which could
possibly relate to this and contribute to the high emotionalism of many of
his works. Could such an undertone even have been evident in the words
of his prize winning song shown on page 43?

With his interest in foreign languages he immensely enjoyed travelling
abroad. Now reckoned to be one of the richest composers in Europe, when
opportunity arose, he would be seen touring on the Continent driving his
Chrysler motor car (one report speaks of him later driving a Rolls Royce
Silver Ghost) with Lottie sitting alongside him - complete with that infamous
rear view mirror and hooter of her own!

In writing of what she called her brother's "passion for foreign
languages", Doris once said, "He would learn a page of vocabulary while he
was shaving, and was delighted when his speeches made on foreign tours
were well received for their accent and vocabulary". She cherished what
she called "a little jeu d'esprit", which he sent to her in later life, of the song
Oh, What a beautiful morning, set to his own words in French, German,
Italian and Russian. His ability in speaking the German language was
noticed by Peter Wiener, an Austrian who once met him. Realising that
Peter came from Austria, Albert immediately began speaking to him in
German, with what Peter called "a slightly Viennese accent", and so well,
that he believed "Albert must have spent some time there". According to
his cousin Dorothy Slanton, referred to in Chapter 2, at some time during
his life Albert "went to Germany to study for a period", and if this be the
case, would be the logical reason why he could speak the language so well.

He was regularly asked to conduct concerts, often devoted to his own
music, by several European orchestras, notably in Holland, Belgium,
France, Germany and Switzerland, including the famous Concertgebouw of
Amsterdam and the Kursaal Grand Symphony Orchestra of Ostend. At
these concerts, for which he was to receive several rave reviews, his ability
to converse with both artists and audiences alike was a factor which
probably contributed to him becoming very popular on the Continent. For
generations many people on the Continent had considered England to be
"The Land without Music", and it was perhaps their liking of his light
amusing music which led them to give him the title "The English
Strauss"[19], which they sometimes called him as his career progressed.

---

[19] Some may argue that this was the title accredited to Archibald Joyce (1873 - 1963) who indeed wrote far more
waltzes than Ketèlbey. These beautiful waltzes including *Dreaming* and *A Thousand Kisses* were however more in
the style of Emile Waldteufel (1837 - 1915) of *The Skaters Waltz* fame, and so more correctly Joyce was often
referred to as "The English Waldteufel".

He particularly liked Monte Carlo and Nice (see plate 42) on the French Riviera, and the coastal resort of Biarritz in Bèarn (in the south west of France) and one of his favourite hotels was the exclusive Negresco in Nice. On his trips abroad he would sometimes combine leisure with concert tours and would take along his cine-film camera and pursue his hobby whenever he could. On one occasion when in Biarritz, he and Lottie took an excursion over to Northern Spain, where he filmed of all things a bullfight, which it was said became one of his prized films.

All of this paints a picture of a lifestyle of luxury and grandeur, but this is not an altogether accurate picture, for whilst they certainly lived fully the life of style when abroad, this was not always the case when on home ground. Yes - he enjoyed doing his concert tours here, entertaining his fans and meeting socially those conductors of municipal orchestras who had become his friends; as too he enjoyed a good unsophisticated party with the Siegenberg family on those Sunday mornings and on New Year's Eve, or welcoming other close musical friends and associates to his Hampstead home at other times. And yet as much as he took to the atmosphere of London life, for the main part of the time when he was there, nothing gave him more pleasure than to be at home with Lottie, working on his compositions at his Victorian writing desk or playing billiards. This "homebird" side of the man was a genuine part of his character, whereby he found simple contentment in the peace and quiet, and even solitude, of the Hampstead home he cherished so much. This he put before mixing in the "right circles" on the London social scene for which, perhaps even to his detriment, he had no interest at all.

With the provincial concerts continuing to be as popular as ever, in August 1927 alone he conducted concerts of his music with the BBC London Wireless Orchestra and the Municipal Orchestras of Harrogate, Margate, Folkestone and Bournemouth. His *Chal Romano Overture* was particularly acclaimed at all of these concerts, and the Margate concert was reported as a particular success with a sell out audience of over 2500 packed into every corner of the Winter Gardens, and at which even before reaching the rostrum, Ketèlbey received an enormous ovation. Several encores followed this concert, one of which was another new work *By the Blue Hawaiian Waters - Tone Picture*. This had been received with much enthusiasm by the audience when played earlier in the concert, and went on to rank amongst his most popular works of the times.

KETELBÈY'S LONDON RESIDENCES

1889 - 1896   8 QUEEN SQUARE, BLOOMSBURY, WC1.
                 (Alfred Hoare's home)

1898 - 1906   13 BRUTON STREET, MAYFAIR, W1.

1906 - 1909   42 (UPPER) BEDFORD PLACE, BLOOMSBURY WC1.

1909 - 1914   73 WEST CROMWELL ROAD, EARL'S COURT, SW5.

1914 - 1921   57 SPRINGFIELD ROAD, ST. JOHN'S WOOD, NW8.

1921 - 1925   15 FROGNAL, HAMPSTEAD, NW3.

1925 - 1947   15 LINDFIELD GARDENS, HAMPSTEAD, NW3.

1947 - 1948   HENDON HALL HOTEL, HENDON, NW4.
                 (London Base)

CHAPTER 8

KETÈLBEY'S DECADE - PART THREE
THE CRITICS AND CONFLICTS OF THE HEART

No man is worthy to succeed until he is willing to fail.
Aiden W. Tozer.

Most critics are just spectators, not players.
Robert Gass.

*J*n the midst of all success, more often than not adversity shows its face, almost as if a levelling force and character forming fact of life, and so was it to be for Mr. Ketèlbey.

One upset came when he was caught up in a legal case over copyright between the composer Frederick W. Austin (1872 - 1952) and Columbia Graphophone Company, which became known as the "Polly Case". Austin had written a ballad opera *Polly* - based on the simple ballad airs in the opera of the same name previously written by the famous English poet and dramatist John Gay (1685 - 1732). Austin had had much success with this new work at London theatres, and so it had become very popular. He had given first right of production of records to The Gramophone Company (HMV) and so in an effort to maximise benefit from the popularity of the opera, Columbia asked Ketèlbey to write his own version of *Polly* based on the same airs used by John Gay, which they then produced on records before The Gramophone Company. Upon hearing this music, Austin was of the opinion that much of it was a copy of his own and so sued Columbia.

The complexity of the case meant that the prolonged court room deliberations went on for some three weeks in July 1923, and were to involve some famous names from the world of music to give their expert opinions, including on behalf of the plaintiff Sir Hugh Percy Allen - Director of the Royal College of Music, Mr. Geoffrey Shaw - composer, and Mr. Ernest Newman - the well-known musical critic; and on behalf of the defendant Sir Dan Godfrey and Mr. Hamilton Harty - famous conductors of the day, Sir

Frederick Bridge - a celebrated organist, and Mr. George H. Clutsam[20] - composer. The whole affair did little for the goodwill of either party, but Columbia were judged to have infringed copyright and were served injunctions and costs, and Ketèlbey who was their main witness - and of course the composer at fault - probably came off worst, in providing additional fuel for his critics.

Another upset and perhaps one of lasting consequence concerned the Performing Right Society, with whom in the early 1920s there arose a dispute over the distribution of funds to its members. In essence the problem was due to its somewhat complicated and ambiguous rules of classification at that time. The more serious classical composers were receiving more income from the Society than those who were writing in a lighter vein, even though this 'lighter music' was being performed more frequently because of its increasing popularity.

The dispute dragged on for some time, and again Ketèlbey got involved in some interesting, jovial and sometimes heated discourses within the letters pages of the musical press. The unfairness of it all, however, annoyed Ketèlbey to the point that in 1926 he actually resigned his membership. After some persuasion he rejoined the Society, following which the whole basis of rules was reviewed and the disparity eventually put right, to the advantage of those who had previously 'missed out' and the disadvantage of those 'more serious' composers. It is said that this in turn led to some signs of professional jealousy and some unfair criticism of Ketèlbey's music by other composers and critics alike. The critic Ariel in referring to his music as being naive and 'slating' its quality to the extreme, went on to refer to "inexpensive pseudo - orientism" contained within *In a Persian Market*, which he farcically said was "Bad music without skill or convincing quality of any kind". It was further apparent that in writing his article in Wireless Notes of *The Musical Times* in November 1926, Ariel was annoyed almost to the point of peevishness when referring to the fact that on one particular evening the music of Ketèlbey was played on the radio for an hour, whereas the night before the music of Vaughan Williams, on the day of his birthday, was only played for fifteen minutes. This fact in itself highlights how popular Ketèlbey had become by the mid 1920s which in no way demeans Vaughan Williams, who at the same time it was rightly said by the *Radio Times* "occupied one of the highest places in British music".

---

20 George Howard Clutsam (1866 - 1951) the Australian born composer who came to England in 1889, and possibly befriended Ketèlbey through his own involvement in the music for silent movies. He wrote several light orchestral pieces, theatrical musicals and with the singer and composer Richard Tauber, composed the music for the film *Heart's Desire*. He wrote many songs, some of which became very popular, including *I know of Two Bright Eyes* and *Ma Curly Headed Babby* - the latter being made famous by the singer Paul Robeson.

Likewise in objectively analysing reviews of recordings of his music in *The Gramophone*, it was apparent that many of the critics were out to derogate the man and deride much of his music. In reading through these for the years from 1926 to 1930, of which there were record reviews of an assortment of his musical works, 76% could be said to be in the category 'fair to good' and 24% in the category 'bad'. Whilst on the face of it one may say that statistically that is not bad going, when one reads the extent of sarcasm and ridicule added to about a third of those 'fair to good' revues, plus what was said in the 'bad' revues, in the final analysis the picture is very different.

In terms of selling records, Ketèlbey had the last laugh with these critics, but their detracting comments, of which I list just a few below, hindered his standing with the musical establishment and added much pleasure to the "high-brow" snobs who already had no intention of giving any credit to light music.

November 1926, Columbia - organ recording *In a Monastery Garden*. Artist: G. T. Pattman ".....The alternative title to this piece is Song of the Soul: I should prefer "Song of the Sole" (especially if fried in butter:- as a piece of spiritual music it is distinctly fishy)."

January 1927, Columbia - orchestral recording *Sanctuary of the Heart* and *A Dream of Christmas*. Artist: Ketèlbey conducting Court Symphony Orchestra. "Zoological Gardens music with effects".

February 1927, HMV - orchestral recording *In a Persian Market* and *In a Chinese Temple Garden*. Performed by: International Concert Orchestra. "After [reviewing] the Fifth [Symphony of Beethoven] it is rather a shame to have to come to earth by way of Chinese temple gardens and other paths of Eastern dalliance. .... The giving out of these trivialities by the International Concert Orchestra is highly adequate".

July 1928, Columbia - orchestral recording of five of his most popular pieces plus *Three Fanciful Etchings* and *In a Fairy Realm*. Artist: Ketèlbey and his Concert Orchestra. The critic Peppering states, "In Mr. Ketèlbey's world of successful make-believe there is room for everyone except the musical pedants and snobs", after saying that Columbia's compliment of issuing the seven compositions in their "Masterworks Album Series" was amiably preposterous!

December 1929, Columbia - orchestral recording *Cockney Suite* and *Jungle Drums*. Artist: Ketèlbey and his Concert Orchestra. Here Peppering states that Ketèlbey is "Very lucky" because "His works are recorded under his own supervision regardless of cost". In referring to

Elgar's *Cockaigne* overture in the same article, he then gloatingly says that any reviews of new recordings of Elgar would be above the Miscellaneous heading under which Ketèlbey was normally listed.

In constructive terms, much of this and other criticism was, in reality, sheer nonsense, and the wise resolve would have been to simply treat it with contempt. However, it provoked such deep anger in Ketèlbey that he responded "like a fish taking bait - regardless of the hook!" and regularly put pen to paper in answering critics in the letters pages of the musical press. He was an excellent letter writer who nearly always responded in long hand, and one gets the impression that he enjoyed "giving 'em as good as he got", but unfortunately in so doing he often now overstated his case in the cause of light music, whilst still purporting to pursue his serious ambitions. This in turn just "added fuel to the fire" for the critics, whereby they would accuse him of claiming that his musical achievements were far higher and better than they actually were. In all of this one has to admit that Ketèlbey often seemed to "go over the top" in defending his cause, as if his fame and fortune were not defence enough! As part of his commercial flair, he had earlier started to list on his personal letter headings several significant accolades paid to him by leading record companies and the media, but possibly as a trait from his "fights" with the critics, this list was expanded to the point where a quarter of the width of his letter headings was taken up with what almost added up to a précis of his 'curriculum vitae'! Whilst this probably aided his cause in dealing with the critics, it must have appeared somewhat pathetic and rather arrogant when writing his fine letters to those to whom he had nothing to prove, and who would otherwise have known that in reality arrogance rarely appeared in his character.

I am not sure whether it was wit or paranoia which prompted some of his responses but, even when he was paid compliments as to his potential ability by one critic, he appeared to respond in the negative, as in a letter printed in *Musical Opinion* of September 1928:-

THE CASE FOR THE COMPOSER
Sir, - Your reviewer of gramophone records in the current issue, referring to me and the Ketèlbey Album of Records issued by the Columbia Co., says; "We are not sure that....he could not do still better if he set himself the task." While thanking the reviewer for the implied compliment, I may say at once that I am quite sure I could, if (and this is the point) the welcome from the public and profession (and reviewers) was sufficiently warm to make it worth while for the publisher to publish it; but my experience has been

that the "better" the work, the less chance it has of even earning its cost of production, let alone of earning popularity.

When one considers the heavy cost of production of such work of mine as *Suite Romantique*, *Chal Romano* (overture), *In a Fairy Realm* (suite), and *Three Fanciful Etchings* (suite), it is not surprising that a publisher cannot afford to publish too much "better" work unless there is a possibility of an occasional "best seller" intervening.

Let reviewers (especially) and others pick out and concentrate on a "better" work when they come across one, such as *Three Fanciful Etchings* or *In a Fairy Realm* in the above mentioned album; to refer to these, which were festival works, in the same manner as to *In a Monastery Garden* is undiscriminating and discouraging, if not ridiculous.

A little warm (even hot) approval of some of the "better" works already in existence would do a lot more good than pious expressions of opinion that a composer could write "still better if he set himself the task" in the future. "Jam tomorrow, but never jam today!"

ALBERT W. KETÈLBEY.
Hampstead N.W.3 Aug. 2 1928

(We agree with Mr. Ketèlbey that the two suites he names are musically far in advance of *In a Monastery Garden*, and it is this fact that led us to make the remark for which we are so kindly taken to task. We do not underrate Mr. Ketèlbey's powers because of his aptness in scoring "hits:" it is what every composer worth his salt has always striven to do. None of them is ever satisfied with the admiration of a clique. - YOUR REVIEWER.

Most of these reactions were totally out of character to the private and retiring man that he normally was, and perhaps even more so, as one who was apparently quite apt to often laugh at himself. His youngest sister Doris believed that her brother's inscrutable character was formed in many ways from an 'inner battlefield' of contrary forces and tensions, and of him once said, "He was a typical little man with the big man inside trying to get out". One of these traits was his mixture of spontaneity and reserve, and this mixture no doubt combined to make him the likeable character that he was. Another trait, however, was his mixture of almost self effacement and dignity - the latter of which he was insistent upon maintaining in all circumstances. Yes, he would be the first to put himself down, but could it be that for dignity's sake a stand had to be made against any who would try to ridicule him? One has to have some sympathy for him in this sad saga, for without doubt he was goaded and his music assiduously, even indiscriminately ridiculed, to such a point that even though at the height of fame, ridicule was to become a ghost to his name, and in some strange undeserved way remain as a stigma even until today, whereby those who suffer the ailments of "music snobbery" will have nothing whatsoever to do with his music, regardless of the attainments that it once reached. As one discerning critic of the 1990s put it "There are some people who wouldn't be caught dead listening to Ketèlbey!"

The logical and fair minded man may ask the reason why Ketèlbey's music was hounded to such an extent? Was he "a prophet without honour", for his reputation on the Continent was if anything higher than in his own country, and indeed one prominent Viennese critic once said of his music, that its quality came second only to that of Johann Strauss II and Franz Lehar? Was it because of his association with music for the silent movies, and his long association with variety theatre - branding him almost a musical 'Jekyll and Hyde' - whereby little or none of his music would be given even serious thought? Was it because he had the privilege (or misfortune) of being born in Birmingham? Or could it just possibly be because too many ordinary people grew to love his music? If the latter be true, this could be the equivalent today of much of Lord Andrew Lloyd Webber's music being ridiculed.

Time and reality were to prove Ketèlbey's negative critics losers, however I leave this section with a letter shown on pages 85 and 86, from one of Ketèlbey's old fans - one of several such letters received by William Neve. I do this not for the praise of the maestro, but in order to bring some light-hearted relief to this otherwise dismal subject, and particularly as I believe he would himself have appreciated the enthusiasm, wit and sense of humour of the writer in expressing some values of old.

Having enjoyed close on twenty happy years association with the Columbia Graphophone Co., in 1926 he decided to relinquish his post of Musical Director and Adviser with them, although he agreed to conduct occasionally for them, which he did until 1930. In the years he spent with Columbia, it was once said that he "worked like a giant" in extracting the best from himself and those who played under him and alongside him, and in co-operating fully with the technical advances in recording which were to occur during his time there. He had always seen his post in the gramophone world as a great adventure, and worked painstakingly with colleagues and those around him to improve the quality of recording, giving his full support through the sometimes trying and testing times of transition from acoustic to electric recording, and the development and experimental stages

1. A.W.K. aged 21.

2. Frederick William Ketelbey.
Circa 1860.

3. George Henry Ketelbey.
Circa 1920.

4. Sarah Ann Ketelbey.
Circa 1920.

5. St. Matthias' Church, where George
and Sarah were married and their
children were baptised.

6. Harold George Ketèlbey. 1912.

7. Florence Beatrice Barlow.
(née Ketelbey)

8. Edith Lavinia Rollason.
(née Ketelbey)

9. Doris Mabel Ketelbey.

10. Jean Olivia Penketh.
(née Crawford)

11. Father George with his favourite dance partner - daughter Florence.

12. Old Alma Street on the right looking from the Royal Exchange, Six Ways, showing the typical "2 up 2 down" type of house into which Ketèlbey was born. On the left is Aston High Street. With acknowledgement Dr. Carl Chinn.

13. Alma Street as it is today, looking from what was the junction of Gerrard Street towards Six Ways.

14. First page of the 1888 *Sonata for Pianoforte*.
With acknowledgement Birmingham Library Services.
(Library citation MS2158. 1998/55 Birmingham City Archive.)

15. St. Silas' Church, Lozells.

16. St. Silas' Church, Lozells.

17. St. John's Church, Wimbledon.

18. St. John's Church, Wimbledon.

19. St. John's Church, Wimbledon.

20. Sir Clifford Curzon.
With acknowledgement Decca/John Vickers.

21. Louis Lewis as Mayor of Islington.
With acknowledgement Margaret Lewis.

22. The Siegenberg family home at
121 Highbury New Park, Islington.

23. Auguste Van Biene - the musician who inspired A.W.K. to write
The Phantom Melody.

24. Sheet music cover: *I loved you more than I knew*,
published by Ascherberg, Hopwood & Crew Ltd.

25. Sheet music cover: *In a Monastery Garden*, published by J.H. Larway.
"Reproduced by permission of J.H. Larway/Edwin Ashdown Ltd."

26. Chilworth Friary.

27. Chilworth Friary.

28. Father Edgar Larway.

29. Joseph H. Larway.

30. The Woods, Chilworth Friary.

31. Brother Ninian Arbuckle ofm, Provincial Secretary, Order of Friars Minor, holding the original manuscript of *In a Monastery Garden*.

32.   First page of manuscript: *In a Monastery Garden*.
"Reproduced by permission of J.H. Larway/Edwin Ashdown Ltd".
With additional acknowledgement, Brother Niniam Arbuckle ofm,
Provincial Secretary, Order of Friars Minor, Provincial Curia, East London.

33. A.W.K. as depicted on the sheet music cover: *Tangled Tunes*, published by
Ascherberg, Hopwood & Crew Ltd.

34. A.W.K. Circa 1920.
With acknowledgement Margaret Lewis.

35. Sheet music cover: *In a Persian Market*, published by Bosworth & Co. Ltd.
"Reproduced by permission of Bosworth & Company Ltd., 8/9 Frith Street, London".

36. 15 Lindfield Gardens, Hampstead.

37. 15 Frognall, Hampstead.

38. Hendon Hall Hotel.

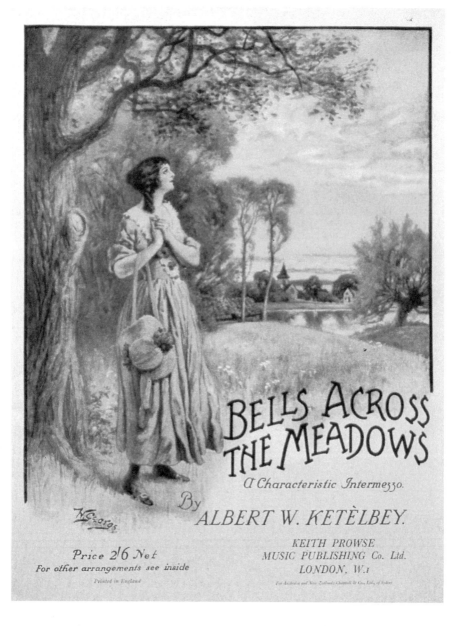

39. Sheet music cover: *Bells across the Meadows*,
published by Keith Prowse & Co. Ltd.

40. New Years Eve Fancy Dress Party, held at 15 Lindfield Gardens 31st December 1928. Theme: "Schooldays". Persons so far identified, from left:- Back row: 6th Catherine Robinson, 8th Louis Lewis Jnr. Middle row: 5th Mrs. G.B. Robinson, 6th A.W.K. 7th Louis Lewis, 8th Mrs. Louis Lewis, 9th Lottie Ketèlbey. Front row: 2nd Teresa Robinson, 3rd Jack Robinson, 6th Dorothy A. Lewis, 8th Clifford Curzon, 7th & 9th the Irish nieces of Mr. & Mrs. G.B. Robinson.

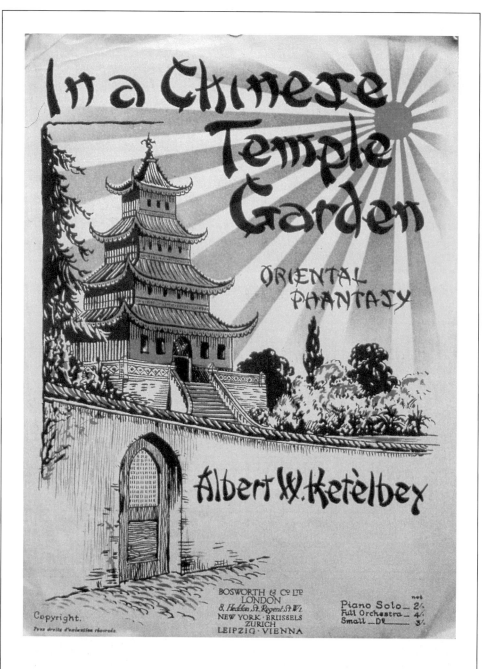

41. Sheet music cover: *In a Chinese Temple Garden*,
published by Bosworth & Co. Ltd.
"Reproduced by permission of Bosworth & Company Ltd., 8/9 Frith Street, London".

42. A.W.K. and Lottie walking along the Esplanade, Nice, France. Circa 1928.

43. George Bainbridge Robinson.

44. 'Uncle Albert' with the Robinson
children, boating on a lake at
Twickenham. Circa 1925.

45. Lieutenant William J. Dunn. 1928.
With acknowledgement Paddy Dunn.

46. Lieutenant Vivian Dunn. 1931.
With acknowledgement Paddy Dunn.

47. A.W.K. with Captain William J. Dunn on the Palace Pier, Brighton.
2nd August 1936.

48. Cover of catalogue: *Albert W. Ketèlbey Popular Piano Music*,
as issued by Bosworth & Co. Ltd.

with all my best wishes,
to Mike and Margaret.
Albert W. Ketèlbey

49. A.W.K. Circa 1948.
With acknowledgement Margaret Lewis.

50. "Rookstone" Bungalow.

51. Osborne Court, Parade, West Cowes, where A.W.K. died at apartment no. 41 on the 26th November 1959.

52. A.W.K. 1959.

Wm. H. Kennon.
14 Newbold Avenue,
Chesterfield.

14.3.75

Dear Mr. Neve,

I am sorry I have taken so long to forward you this personal anecdote but having had recent experience of publishers there is still time, so here goes.

As a boy I spent many delightful holidays at Bridlington in the twenties. Although the rest of the family had a flair and some considerable talent for music, I had to be cajoled into my first concert which was to hear Herman Darewski on the Spa. I was thrilled and immediately converted, but it was a year or two later that I had the opportunity of seeing Ketelbey on the rival plot, the Princes Parade, at the same resort.

It was a Sunday evening and I was somewhat surprised that my mother and father, devout Methodists, should consider taking my sister and myself to a concert on a Sunday. It was billed as a Celebrity Concert, which no doubt salved their consciences but still left me a little perplexed as I had been brought up to 'remember the Sabbath Day' and observe it strictly. Tickets were purchased beforehand, the prices 1/- adults, 6d children.

The resident orchestra was under the direction of Lionel Johns who gave concerts mornings and evenings and sometimes broadcast, regarded as an honour and privilege then. In those days many of the audience read books, did crosswords and ladies did their knitting (not on Sundays) although the clicking of needles occasioned some disdainful looks from other patrons.

During the week I presume the programme was practised and on the day Ketelbey had a full dress rehearsal for the hall was closed to the public. The concert performance took place between 8 & 10 in the evening before a packed house. Of the man himself in charge I recall vividly his terrific energy, gusto and fury. I have often said he thrashed this little orchestra of 15 members, a mixture of strings and wind instruments - please excuse my lack of technicalities. He used his head as well as his arms and baton to symbolise the mood and tempo. With so small a number he could pick on the instrumentalists for any given effect. He spared neither himself nor his men - his vitality and intensity I can still see; he soon became red in the face as you can well imagine. The whole evening was devoted to his work but the piece that I recall most easily was, Bells across the Meadows. I should guess the solo work was done on the vibraphone which together with the xylophone was enjoying great popularity. I marvelled at the versatility of the 'percussion' player for Ketelbey's work makes considerable demands on this member.

At the conclusion of the concert Albert Ketelbey received rapturous applause which he richly deserved. He was magnanimous and shared his glory with the orchestra and Lionel Johns himself whom he called to the rostrum.

I hope you will find something of interest in this rather hasty report. I wish you every success with your work.

Yours sincerely,

W. H. Kennon.

of microphone recording during the 1920s. In this same post with Columbia, being the professional that he was, but also in no small measure due to his kind disposition, he had done much to promote the work on record of many other British composers of light music and popular songs. These include Haydn Wood, Charles Ancliffe, Edward German, Sydney Baynes, Harold Fraser-Simson, Ivor Novello, Wilfrid Sanderson, James Molloy, James Tate, William Squire, Sidney Jones, Thomas Johnson and Guy d'Hardelot; and on the Regal label with the Silver Stars Band, he advanced much the military marches of Major Frederick J. Ricketts (1881 - 1945) - alias Kenneth J. Alford, of *Colonel Bogey* fame. Having become renowned for his own brilliance in orchestration was probably one good reason why Ketèlbey seemed to take a particular interest in Alford's military music for, in his now famous marches, Alford's own brilliance in both band arrangement and counterpoint shines through.

The world fame which came to Ketèlbey truly astonished him, and in his wry style once commented that he "had found fame and fortune in a Monastery Garden", and whilst he always appeared to be unimpressed by such, he did, however, cherish the independence that wealth brought him. By 1928 such was the popularity of his compositions that Columbia came up with the idea of recording his most well-known pieces as albums of authentic composer-recordings - namely "Ketèlbey conducting his Concert Orchestra". So it was that between March 1928 and April 1930, Columbia's old colleague returned to their Clerkenwell Road Studios on several occasions to record 16 of his most popular pieces, which were duly issued with labels bearing the appropriate appellation. These recordings, including one of *The Phantom Melody/Algerian Scene* played as a duet with Ketèlbey on piano and Albert Sandler on the violin, proved to be a great success - regardless of the critics previously referred to. I have heard most of these recordings and from an authentic performance standard can understand why they were so successful, particularly where the maestro himself plays relevant piano parts, as he does with brilliant effect in the recording of his immortal *Wedgwood Blue*. In a very full career within the recording industry, he was to make over 600 recordings of a mixed genre of music on the labels of no less than twenty recording companies in the United Kingdom, besides Columbia, and other companies on the Continent.

The main reason why he relinquished his post with Columbia, was in order to spend more time in the peaceful surroundings of his beloved Hampstead home, where he could devote himself to composition - and even now still apparently undaunted - to continue in his quest of classical music stature.

SPECIAL COLUMBIA ISSUE

ALBERT·W·KETELBEY ALBUM

Conducted & Supervised by the Composer

CONTENTS OF THE ALBUM

Played by Albert W. Ketelbey's Concert Orchestra.

DARK BLUE LABEL—12-inch Double-Sided, Price 4/6 each

9403	In a Monastery Garden — In Two Parts
9404	In a Persian Market — In Two Parts
9405	Sanctuary of the Heart — In Two Parts
9406	THREE FANCIFUL ETCHINGS— A Passing Storm Cloud on a Summer Day / The Ploughman Homeward Plods His Weary Way (Part 1)
9407	The Ploughman Homeward Plods (Part 2) / Quips and Cranks and Wanton Wiles (Scene de Ballet Russe)
9408	Chal Romano—Gipsy Overture — In Two Parts
9409	IN A FAIRY REALM (Suite)— (1) The Moonlit Glade / (2) The Queen Fairy Dances
9410	(3) The Gnomes March / Bells Across the Meadows

Eight Records Complete in Art Album with Interesting Descriptive Notes 36s.

THERE can be none who have not become familiar with the romance and colour introduced into music by the composer of "In a Monastery Garden." Albert W. Ketelbey's music is the music of those who look for pictures to be conjured to the mind through the ear. He is the most popular of all British composers. And this Album of Records of selections of his works brings the composer's own renderings. They include two works—"Three Fanciful Etchings" and "In a Fairy Realm"—now recorded for the first time, each a series of pictures that will give the same delight to his admirers as anything that has gone before, breathing as they do the spirit of romance and imagination.

Columbia advertisement for their new records of "Ketèlbey conducting his Concert Orchestra".

He once said that often snippets of music would come into his mind in all kinds of situations and circumstances, and these he would jot down and keep for possible future use in compositions. He also once commented that in producing some of his most popular pieces he had as he put it "slaughtered the innocents" by using some more serious compositions as the foundation of such pieces, and this indeed may add some truth to the use of the unpublished String Quartet as the basis of *In a Monastery Garden*. Perhaps it was the mourning of such losses, and the knowledge of his father's disappointment in him, which would not leave him but rather continue to make him determined to write and be received in the more serious vein. Is this why, of his popular successes, he once remarked "I hope they will make me enough money so that I can become an amateur and compose **music** once again"?

From what I have unearthed on this aspect of the character of the man, I have gleaned that there was certainly some deep inner conflict within his heart, almost depriving him of a true sense of musical achievement and contentment "with his lot". This has led me to conclude that this was one reason why he loved so much simply being at home with wife Lottie, where he found such immense contentment, which was otherwise wanting or lacking in his musical life. And yet was this colliding of worlds within the man - combining the light heart with the serious - the very essence and attractiveness of his music, so often wherein one minute the heart skips and jumps and smiles, and the next it rests and yearns and cries in serious contemplative mood? It is almost as if sometimes he purported never to really want the particular musical gift and "mantle" which God had given him, but rather - at least in his own mind - something above it and a "mantle" not destined to be his. As brilliant as he was at what he did, it was as if he did not realise that although his music was not 'classical' in the fullest sense of that word, it was most definitely quality light music in a class and of a character all of its own with its brilliant orchestration , and this is what his audiences loved and wanted more of.

What confuses this recurring issue even more and adds more complexity to the character of the man, is the fact that Ketèlbey knew very well that this was what the public wanted, and once wrote when giving his own views as to the reason for his success:-

> ".....I gave the public melody well harmonised and (I think
> I can say) well constructed which is what they want, instead
> of what the "high-brows" think they ought to have. I have
> never been able to see anything derogatory in that, for

a composer (who is, or should be, a business man when his livelihood is concerned) can no more afford to ignore public opinion than the ordinary commercial man can. The same inexorable law of supply and demand operates in each case...."

The publishers and recording companies certainly knew this only too well, and would not concede to his 'hidden agenda', but simply encouraged him to persist in writing the expressive and tuneful pieces the great British public wanted to hear - for they had most definitely already put their "label" on him. It seems ironical - even sad - that whereas "The Waltz King" Johann Strauss II realised his musical gift and so his destiny at an early age, "The English Strauss" Albert W. Ketèlbey (if I can be permitted to call him that) did not, or did not appear to realise his until he was in middle age. It was not until this time when in his early fifties that he truly relinquished his serious music ambitions, when after some persuasion, perhaps reluctantly but graciously - if not humorously - he agreed to make light music composition his top priority, and lay aside those serious aspirations.

As if to confirm this he produced such pieces as *By the Blue Hawaiian Waters*, *A Dream of Christmas* and his light-hearted and comical *Jungle Drums - Patrol*, and in 1928 published his *Suite - In a Fairy Realm* - its three movements being *The Moonlit Glade, The Queen-Fairy Dances* and *The Gnomes March*. This suite had in fact been given its first performance at the Harrogate Musical Festival of September 1927, and another *Suite - Three Fanciful Etchings*, which was also published in 1928, had been performed for the first time at the Bournemouth Musical Festival of April 1927. Both of these works had been well received, although both were yet again bearing his penship of more serious music! However, the second movement of *Three Fanciful Etchings*, which is rather pastoral in character and entitled *The Ploughman Homeward Plods his Weary Way*, brings out again his sheer brilliance in painting musical pictures, where the eye can clearly see 'exactly' in the music, what the title implies. The other two movements in this suite are entitled *A Passing Storm Cloud on a Summers Day* and *Quips and Cranks and Wanton Wiles*. Some regard *Three Fanciful Etchings*, which is quite "Elgarian" in style, as one of his finest compositions, and in referring to it, and Ketèlbey's pursuit of serious musicianship, H. C. Burgess once said of his friend, "He was a likeable soul, a clever man and one who has left his mark on the nation's music. Tho' mightily pleased with the financial results of his most popular compositions,

I think that Ketèlbey himself, would have preferred to be remembered by his more serious works.......He remained an unspoilt man, spoke a musicians "language" and didn't object when I twitted him upon the "simplicity" of most of his orchestral music, which made such little demand on the techniques of players that they lost interest......Later he sent me parts of an Overture and a Suite called *Three Fanciful Etchings*, which were quite difficult enough to make most of us keep awake!"

The year 1929 brought forth *The Sacred Hour - Reverie* with organ and chorus, the success of which was such that the initial volume of sales of sheet music was far greater than any other piece he had previously written, although today it is not included amongst his popular compositions. He recorded this work with Columbia in April 1929, and in the summer of the same year he undertook an exhausting but most successful European tour, combining concert performance and broadcasting of his works at major radio stations, including those in Amsterdam, Brussels, Lille, Lyon, Zurich, Berlin, Leipzig, Munich and Budapest. At such concerts abroad he would be as meticulous as ever - if not more so than when on home ground - as regards the interpretation and performance of his works, and would go to great lengths in rehearsals to explain to the orchestra the essence and content of the work in hand, thereby moulding his conception and motivating those special nuances each work required.

CHAPTER 9

CONCERTS GALORE, THE MILITARY AND
COMPOSITION TO THE PLEASURE OF THE KING!

.....If you can talk with crowds and keep your virtue,
Or walk with Kings - nor lose the common touch.....

Rudyard Kipling.

*T*he wise man once said, "I will not trail my weariness along the highways of defeat", words true of Ketèlbey, because regardless of his setbacks and the scorn of his critics during the 1920s, unabashed he continued on his musical journey. His success had however brought with itself a rather paradoxical difficulty to almost a fear of "diminishing returns", due to the market becoming "saturated" and his music heard to the point of surfeit - *In a Persian Market* being a perfect example. In order to avert such loss he had made use of pseudonyms as a marketing tool, and indeed he was quite a dab hand in the use of these. As we have seen, in the tail end of his days at Trinity College of Music, when his aspirations were for recognition as a serious composer, he had used the name Raoul Clifford for his lighter (mainly mandolin) compositions. The Russian sounding Anton Vodorinski, he had first used to wisely disguise his identity when setting piano lessons as an examiner for Trinity College, notably in his *Six Original Pieces without Octaves Op. 9*. With the success of such pieces as *The Phantom Melody*, *In a Monastery Garden*, *In the Moonlight*, etc., came the realisation of his real name being associated with this music of the lighter idiom, and therefore he used again the Anton Vodorinski name for some of his more serious piano compositions, publishing these with French titles and an opus number, which seemed to work well for him. As he became acknowledged as a brilliant orchestrator of his light popular pieces, so he exploited this reputation when in arranging some of his Vodorinski serious piano pieces for orchestra, he had them published as "Composed by Anton Vodorinski; orchestrated by Albert W. Ketèlbey".

And so at the height of fame in the 1920s, one has to admire his commercial acumen when he made use of the pseudonym medium in an attempt to defeat any adverse market conditions, and in this context had also been born "Geoffrey Kaye", "A.William Aston", and the grand "Andre de Basque".

Interestingly, as early as 1915, for a comic piece he composed called *Fiddle Fun* for piano and violin, and recorded under the Regal label, the performers are listed as 'Louis and Lewis' - being the first names respectively of his oldest brother-in-law and his father-in-law, which as far as I am aware were used by Ketèlbey purely as pseudonym names, and indeed the pianist on this recording could well have been himself! It should be said, however, that with the exception of his serious piano music published under the Vodorinski name (several pieces of which I have previously referred to), and *A Musical Jig-Saw* and similar *Christmas* potpourri published under the Aston name, nothing of any real and lasting significance was published under the other pseudonyms which he used.

His next success was *The Clock and the Dresden Figures*, which he dedicated "To my friend, Lieut. W.J. Dunn, MC.", and at its first performance at the Kingsway Hall on the 8th February 1930 with the composer at the piano, such was the appreciation and ovation of the audience to the piece, that it was immediately performed again from beginning to end! This was to be the last piece he recorded with Columbia in April 1930, with his *Wedgwood Blue* on the reverse side, and was to become one of his most broadcast compositions of the 1930s.

The year 1931 started well with a successful Ketèlbey concert in January, again at the Kingsway Hall, and on 11th April he received rapturous applause following a performance of his works with the Municipal Orchestra at the Pavilion, Bournemouth, which included two new works in *The Vision of Fuji-San - Prelude* and *Knights of the King - Grand March*, the latter which he dedicated to the Royal Horse Guards, presenting their Band with a Conductor Part inscribed "Specially composed for and dedicated to Lieut-Colonel A.E. TURNOR, MC, and the Regiment of His Majesty's Royal Horse Guards (The Blues)".

The summer of 1931 was to include a packed schedule of his popular concerts, one being at Weymouth on 2nd August 1931, and so popular a celebrity was he now, that this could be summed up by a report on this particular concert, which appeared in *The Sound Wave* for September 1931, as follows:-

Encore Ketèlbey!

Once again the popular composer-conductor, Albert W. Ketèlbey, has been on the musical warpath during the month, conducting special "All Ketèlbey" Concerts at (among other places) Margate, Weymouth, Bridlington, Bexhill, etc.

We were present on August 2 at his concert at the Winter Gardens, Margate, and never have we seen the building so packed; official information gives the audience at over 2,700, although the hall is only supposed to hold 2,000 when full! Staircases and every corner (even the terrace outside) were crammed to suffocation with an eager and responsive audience that literally *ate* every note of Ketèlbey's works, and gave him an overwhelming ovation after every number.

The performance by Mr. Herbert Lodge's fine Municipal Orchestra, led by Mr. Leonard Hirsch (of the Halle Orchestra), under the magnetic baton of Mr. Ketèlbey, was vivid in the extreme, the standard of execution and the *nuances* and general flexibility being of absolutely symphonic excellence, and what was more remarkable, this performance was obtained (as Mr. Ketèlbey told the audience afterwards) *without a rehearsal of any kind!* - so much confidence did Mr. Ketèlbey have in the quality of the players under him.

It was really a great night, and emphasises once more the fact that Ketèlbey's marvellous popularity is no flash-in-the-pan success, but is undoubtedly more deeply rooted than ever, and that every new number Ketèlbey composes, unceasingly adds to his success and world-renown.

Also in the same year was published another evergreen in the form of *In the Mystic Land of Egypt*, with its beautiful, haunting main theme, and the final section of which, I believe, in its version for full orchestra with solo voice and chorus, expresses Ketèlbey at his absolute best, and herein is surely heard some influence of Charles Gounod (1818 - 1893) for whose music it is believed Ketèlbey had much admiration. The solo and chorus are referred to here in singing optional words he set to the piece in his typical romantic style:-

"O maid of beauteous tresses,
And eyes of soft caresses,
Your glance is all beguiling,
And your lips are ever smiling,
Let us float together
For ever and for ever,
To some far distant isle,
A-down the mystic Nile".

The good fortune of the silent movie era, with its corresponding demand for sheet music, was to last until the famous onslaught of *The Jazz Singer* in 1929 - and so to films incorporating their own sound track. The increasing popularity of gramophone and radio had slowly but surely taken its toll on the sale of sheet music, and particularly that of light music, bearing in mind that until these listening mediums had come on the scene, two of the main forms of entertainment at home were 'parlour' piano playing and the singing of 'drawing-room' ballads. The latter Ketèlbey had capitalised on in his own song compositions, and also in adding words to his successful orchestral compositions, notably *In a Monastery Garden* and *Bells across the Meadows*, but the demise of these two mediums of home entertainment was hastened, at least in some part, by the fashionable dance music of the "Roaring Twenties".

The effect of "talkies" on the demand for "cinema music" had devastating - and almost overnight - repercussions on publishers and composers alike, not to mention the thousands of musicians who were to lose their jobs. Ketèlbey was fortunate, however, in this respect, for although "talkies" obviously had their effect on him, with his continuing popularity and so inclusion within the realms of radio and gramophone, he was to very much "gain on the roundabouts what he had lost on the swings". It is interesting to note here that not all cinema orchestras were killed off with the coming of "talkies" in 1929, as some of these had by now become concert orchestras in their own right, and were to continue providing their own musical entertainment apart from the movies, indeed some growing after "talkies" to become larger force orchestras.

The continuing and increasing popularity of radio as a listening and relaxation medium by the masses in the 1930s, regardless of the depression, was again to contribute significantly to the success of the new compositions of Ketèlbey.

By 1932 the number of radio licence holders had risen to five million (said then to represent a potential audience of some 25 million), and this was to rise to nine million licences held by the late 1930s. When one bears in mind that at this time the performances of popular light music concerts at music halls, town halls, seaside pavilions and cinemas all over the country were regularly broadcast live on radio, besides the playing of an ever increasing library of records, it is easy to see that the vast majority of the population were regular radio listeners to his music. Such was the popularity and success of the 'lad from Brum' on the radio waves, that in one year well over 1500 broadcasts of his music were made, besides an average 50 broadcasts each month by continental radio stations, so adding to his continued success in Europe. One of these continental stations, Radio Luxembourg, was broadcasting a programme of concert music each Sunday afternoon sponsored by Decca. Ketèlbey composed the signature tune for this programme entitled *Sunday Afternoon Reverie*, the melody being cleverly based on the notes D E C C A, and which bore the dedication "an appreciation of the Decca Sunday radio concerts".

Consistent with the popularity of the radio with the masses was also the continued development and use of the gramophone - another contributing factor to the fame of Ketèlbey, whose music was now being regularly recorded. Through the changes wrought by electrical recording and playback, with electric motors, pick-ups and loudspeakers replacing wind-up motors, sound boxes and acoustic horns, there had come on the scene cabinet radiograms, for those who could afford this new "fashionable furniture". There were some executives in the gramophone record industry who believed that the increasing use of radio by the masses would lead to increased sales of records, but however, the opposite proved true, and in fact as more radios were purchased in the 1930s so there appeared to be a correlating decline in record sales. In response to this, and in an effort to regain record sales Columbia were to lead the industry in developing an electric record player which operated through a mains radio, which they were to eventually launch in 1938 without profit, at just 39/6d (£1.98),so bringing this listening medium within the budgets of an increasing number of ordinary working folk, which in turn was to mean even more sales of Ketèlbey's popular music on records.

When in London he now worked mainly from home, each year appearing to the public when he continued with concert tours of his music, throughout the country, and in *Musical Opinion* of September 1932 it was reported that:- "......the success attending the "Ketèlbey" concerts this season has been far greater than any before". Roy Douglas, then a member of Folkestone Municipal Orchestra, remembered Ketèlbey conducting a concert

Another of Bosworth & Co.'s full page advertisements. October 1936.
"Reproduced by permission of Bosworth & Company Ltd. 8/9 Frith Street, London."

of his works at Leas Cliff Hall in Folkestone at about this time, and particularly recalled how meticulous and enthusiastic a conductor he was, saying, "He rehearsed his works as solemnly and carefully as if they were by Beethoven or Mozart". Indeed Ketèlbey's continuing enthusiasm was confirmed by Frank Walker, who when speaking of visiting him at his Hampstead home in connection with Ketèlbey appearing on The Frank Walker Octet's regular Saturday evening broadcast for the BBC said, "When I visited his home he would sit down at the piano - and did not stop playing throughout the whole of my visit - bubbling over with enthusiasm".

In the summer of 1932 at a concert at the Winter Gardens, Margate, with Ketèlbey at the piano, there had been played for the first time his new work for solo piano and orchestra *Dance of the Merry Mascots*, following the applause for which it was again repeated in its entirety, and was to become another popular radio piece. Later in that year he conducted no less than eight concerts of his music during a tour of Holland, including on 29th September 1932 a 'sell out' concert in Amsterdam at the height of the tour, conducting the Concertgebouw Orchestra and a mass choir of one hundred and sixty voices. On the night of this concert the only vacant seat in the Concertgebouw was the one reserved for the duty policeman! The reports of his success and popularity on the Continent, which were regularly high-lighted by Bosworth & Co. in their advertisements in the musical press, could not but fuel and increase even further his popularity here, to the point that the Ketèlbey Festival Concert of 10th February 1934 at the Kingsway Hall was reported in the *Musical Opinion* of March 1934 as ".... an increasingly successful annual function ....played to an audience of two thousand ....whose appreciation after hearing his best known pieces was overwhelming.......".

The most popular of these best known pieces was of course *In a Monastery Garden*, and the success of this had been further enhanced when the popular Australian born bass-baritone singer Peter Dawson (1882 - 1961) had recorded the work as a song on the H.M.V. label in November 1932. Peter Dawson was to make use of other Ketèlbey songs in his repertoire, and another entertainer, who was to later make use of the success of *In a Monastery Garden* and also *Bells across the Meadows*, was Ronnie Ronalde (born 1923 and now living in New Zealand) the renown 'Whistler', for whom *In a Monastery Garden* was to become his familiar signature tune on radio and television during the 1950s. Also in the late 1920s and well into the 1930s, the success of both *In a Monastery Garden* and *In a Persian Market* were to be even further enhanced, when in 1926 the brilliant organist Reginald Foort - renown for his popular recitals on the BBC Theatre Organ - made a famous recording of these pieces playing the New Gallery Cinema Organ, on the HMV label (C1285), which achieved substantial record sales.

The regular orchestra at the Kingsway Hall Festival Concerts was that of the Royal Horse Guards, "The Blues", with the Kingsway Hall Choral Society (of a hundred and fifty voices) and Mr. Alan Brown, the celebrated organist and Musical Director of the Kingsway Hall, on the four - manual organ. The regular co-conductor and assistant to Ketèlbey was Lieutenant William J. (Paddy) Dunn M.C.(1875 - 1937)(see plate 45), later Captain W. J. Dunn M.V.O., M.C., p.s.m., Director of Music, Royal Horse Guards (1927 - 35). He was the father of Lieutenant Vivian Dunn (1908 - 1995)(see plate 46), Director of Music, Royal Marines (1931 - 53), who was also to co-conduct and assist Ketèlbey at several of his concerts and 'step in his father's shoes' at these Kingsway Hall events after 1935. Lieutenant Vivian Dunn was to become Captain M.V.O., and later Lieutenant-Colonel C.V.O., O.B.E., F.R.A.M. and Principal Director of Music, Royal Marines, (1953 - 68) in which capacity he himself wrote several fine marches, including *Soldiers of the Sea, Captain General, Cockleshell Heroes* and *The Pompey Chimes* - dedicated to Portsmouth Football Club. In 1969 he became Sir Vivian Dunn K.C.V.O., O.B.E., F.R.A.M., Hon G.S.M., F.R.S.A., R.M., when he was knighted for his services to the military, and he is of course now a famous name in the annals of the military band world, and particularly that associated with the Royal Marines. Both 'Paddy' and Vivian, as they were known to him, were to become close friends of Ketèlbey, and as such frequent visitors to his Hampstead home. Indeed his friendship with Paddy went back to their student days, and over the years they built up a very good rapport with each other, quite often "pulling each others leg", Paddy often referring to his friend as "Albert the Monk" - the connotation obviously relating to his famous work, and in responsive mood Albert would often retort by calling him "Paddybert". Such was his warmth and admiration towards Ketèlbey, that in an interview article which appeared in *The Southend Standard* in August 1935, in connection with a Carnival Drumhead Service to be held in Chalkwell Park, Southend, in which he was to conduct the Band of the Royal Horse Guards, he said, "I believe the music specially played for the occasion, *Judex* by Gounod, and the *Sanctuary of the Heart*, by Ketèlbey, will be fully appreciated. I may mention that Albert Ketèlbey is my greatest personal friend. I have known him since he was a young student, and all his works have been tried over by 'The Blues'".

In the early 1930s the Band of the Royal Horse Guards under the direction of Lieutenant W.J. Dunn, were to become popular performers at concerts in halls and on bandstands and piers, etc., all over the country, and gave many concerts at the old Bingley Hall in Birmingham during this time, with Lieutenant Dunn becoming a popular personality with Birmingham audiences - perhaps in no short measure due to him always making special mention of, and regularly playing the music of his Birmingham born friend Albert W. Ketèlbey.

Early in 1934 the composition for pizzicato strings and celeste entitled *My Lady Brocade* was published, and in the November 1934 issue of the *Musical Opinion*, following another successful concert tour, taking in Margate, Bournemouth, Bath, Bridlington, Blackpool, New Brighton and Liverpool, it was reported that, "THE TRIUMPHAL MARCH of the popular composer Albert W. Ketèlbey still continues....". The heart of Ketèlbey now, however - regardless of these successful concert tours - was in his home, where at his favourite well-worn Victorian writing desk he could compose at leisure, and as an extremely patriotic man the knowledge that the King and Queen appreciated his music must have pleased him immensely.

The year 1932 had seen Ketèlbey's first association with Royalty when he published *A Birthday Greeting - Intermezzo*, with a dedication printed on the head as follows:-

> "Composed in honour of the birthday of HRH the Princess Elizabeth of York, to whom, by special permission it is most respectfully dedicated.   April 21st 1932".

Another recorded acquaintance with Royalty speaks well of his popularity with such, when following the playing of his march *A State Procession* from the *Cockney Suite* as an accompaniment to the arrival of King George V and Queen Mary for the Royal Command Variety Performance at the London Palladium on the 8th May 1934, the King asked specially if it could be repeated during the interval. This, and the fact that the King and Queen remained in the Royal Box to listen to it "with great pleasure", led to Ketèlbey being announced in the *Birmingham Evening Despatch* of 9th May 1934 as "the happiest man in England". Although not present for the performance, he was reported as saying, "It was very gracious indeed of the King, and I am naturally delighted", and further that "It is gratifying to know one of my tunes has pleased their Majesties". Of the star line up included for this Royal Variety Performance, were George Robey, Elsie and Doris Waters, and Arthur Lucan - of "Old Mother Riley" fame. The last association of *A State Procession* with Royalty was in 1961, when at the Trooping the Colour ceremony on Horse Guards Parade in celebration of Her Majesty's Birthday, it was included as the first item in The March Past (In Slow Time).

THE KING'S REQUEST

AT THE ROYAL COMMAND VARIETY PERFORMANCE

A STATE PROCESSION

(Buckingham Palace)

BY

ALBERT W. KETÈLBEY

(From "A Cockney Suite"—Cameos of London Life)

At the Royal Command Variety Performance (London Palladium—May 8th, 1934) " A State Procession " (Buckingham Palace), which was played as an Overture to the programme, was repeated during the interval at the King's request

---

MORNING POST

THE 'COMMAND' PERFORMANCE
Overture Repeated at the King's Request

After Henry Hall and his B.B.C. Orchestra had closed the first part the King specially asked for the overture to be repeated by the Palladium Orchestra. Owing to the Royal party being a few minutes late he had missed hearing it.

It was taken from Ketèlbey's "Cockney Suite" and represented a State procession with the King and Queen going to open Parliament and regimental bands playing as they passed along the route.

The King expressed his very great pleasure in hearing these reminiscences of scenes peculiarly familiar to him.

DAILY MIRROR

When their Majesties entered the flower-decked Royal Box the King consulted his programme and found that the overture had already been played.

This was "A State Procession" (Buckingham Palace), by Ketèlbey, and depicts the King and Queen going to open Parliament in State.

At the end of the first half his Majesty asked that this piece should be repeated instead of the intermission music set down in the programme. Told that this would lengthen the programme by a few minutes, the King smiled and said he should be only too glad to wait.

Afterwards, when he thanked the management, he said that he had enjoyed the musical selection very much.

DAILY SKETCH

ROYAL REQUEST
Orchestra Play Overture Again for Their Majesties

Henry Hall and his B.B.C. dance orchestra brought the first part of the programme to a close.

There was then a surprise request from the Royal Box.

The King and Queen, who arrived after the overture had been played, asked that it should be repeated during the interval instead of the pieces originally selected—a sure indication that their Majesties were enjoying the entertainment.

The overture was "A State Procession" (Buckingham Palace), from Ketèlbey's "Cockney Suite."

DAILY TELEGRAPH

THE KING'S REQUEST

During the interval, the King sent a message to ask that the "State Procession" Overture from Ketèlbey's "Cockney Suite" which has been played before his arrival, should be repeated. This piece is a musical description of a King and Queen driving from Buckingham Palace to open Parliament, and their Majesties remained in the Royal box to listen to it.

BIRMINGHAM EVENING DESPATCH

THE MUSIC THE KING LIKED
Ketèlbey's "Cockney Suite."

Repeated Overture.   Birmingham Born Composer.

PIANO SOLO Price 2/-
Brass Band 3/-   Reed & Brass Band 3/6

Included in the Orchestration of the complete "Cockney Suite"

Full Orchestra 10/-   Small Orchestra 7/6   Military Band 21/-

Recorded on Columbia Records 9860/1/2 by Albert W. Ketèlbey and his Concert Orchestra of which "The Daily Telegraph" says "A delicious Suite"

BOSWORTH & Co., Ltd., 8, Heddon Street, Regent Street, London, W.1

Publicity sheet for *A State Procession*, issued by Bosworth & Co.
"Reproduced by permission of Bosworth & Company Ltd., 8/9 Frith Street, London."

𝔓rogramme of 𝔐usic

To be performed by

The Mounted Band of the Life Guards, The Massed Bands, Drums and Pipes of the Brigade of Guards

at the celebration of

Her Majesty's Birthday

ON THE HORSE GUARDS PARADE AT 11 A.M. ON THURSDAY, JUNE 11TH, 1953

———

Lieutenant-Colonel & Director of Music A. Lemoine, The Life Guards.

Major & Director of Music F. J. Harris, M.B.E., A.R.C.M., Grenadier Guards.

Major & Director of Music D. A. Pope, A.R.C.M., Coldstream Guards.

Lieutenant-Colonel & Director of Music S. Rhodes, M.B.E., Mus. Bac., A.R.C.M., Scots Guards (Senior Director of Music, Brigade of Guards).

Captain & Director of Music C. H. Jaeger, Mus. Bac., L.R.A.M., A.R.C.M., Irish Guards.

Captain & Director of Music F. L. Statham, L.R.A.M., A.R.C.M., Welsh Guards.

———

Royal Salute   ...   "God Save the Queen"

INSPECTION OF THE LINE

Slow March	...	"With Honour Crowned"	...	...	*Ketelbey*
Quick March	...	"Long Live Elizabeth"	...	...	*German*

18

Page of programme for Trooping the Colour ceremony. 1953.

He returned again to the genre of more serious music for two other Royal occasions, firstly in 1935 when he wrote the march *With Honour Crowned* in which he uses with much panache his favourite tubular bells, composed in honour of the Silver Jubilee of King George V. Following an initial Court performance played before the Royal Family at Windsor Castle by the Band of the Royal Horse Guards under Lieutenant Dunn, it was given its first public performance by the same Band, but under the baton of the composer at one of the popular Ketèlbey Festival Concerts at the Kingsway Hall held on 9th February 1935. It was then played to the King at the Jubilee Thanksgiving Service at St. Paul's Cathedral on 6th May 1935, and again during Trooping the Colour in that same year. I believe that this is the finest march Ketèlbey wrote, and of it Sir Vivian Dunn once said, "upon writing *With Honour Crowned*, the composer was immensely enthusiastic about it, playing it at every opportune moment, whereby in 1935 it seemed to be played over and over again". Although rarely featured in military pageants and parades today, *With Honour Crowned* remained popular with the military up to the 1950s, and in both 1952 and 1953 at Trooping the Colour it was chosen as the Slow March to be played whilst Queen Elizabeth inspected the parade. Secondly in 1937 he wrote *Royal Cavalcade - New Coronation Grand March*, composed in honour of the then forthcoming coronation of George VI, although this did not have anywhere near the same impact as *With Honour Crowned*.

Ketèlbey's music had now long been very popular with military bands who regularly included it in their repertoire at concert hall and band stand concerts and at military tattoos, and in fact as early as 1920 and 1921 when *In a Persian Market* and *Bells across the Meadows* had been published, many of them had seized upon the novelty of these pieces, to include them, very often as encores, in such concerts and tattoos. Several of these bands, including the Royal Horse Guards Band, H.M. Coldstream Guards Band and Massed Bands made recordings of their performances of his music. So it was that they seized hold of these new 'Royal' march compositions for prestigious use within their programmes, and at the Aldershot Military Tattoos for the years 1935 to 1938 Ketèlbey's military music played a prominent part in the pageants and displays, performed at these by the Massed Bands of over 1000 musicians and duly recorded and produced on record. His marches included in the programmes were:-

1935   Item 8. Pageant "Long Live the King" Part III SILVER JUBILEES. March: *A State Procession*. (from *Cockney Suite*).

1936   Item 9. Pageant "The First Prince of Wales, The Legend of Edward of Caernarvon". ENTRY OF THE KING'S PROCESSION. March:*With Honour Crowned*.

1937   Item 10. Pageant "The Challenge". ENTRY OF THE BODY-GUARDS AND BANNER BEARERS. March: *Royal Cavalcade*.

1938   Item 1. Pageant "The Field of Cloth of Gold. The arrival of King Henry VIII of England at his camp, and the passing of King Francois I of France on his way to his camp at Ardres". THE PROCESSIONS. March: *A State Procession*. (from *Cockney Suite*).

Knights of the King was to also remain quite a popular march with the military, and for the Military Musical Pageants held at Wembley Stadium in 1971, Lieutenant Colonel Trevor Le M. Sharpe O.B.E., L.R.A.M., A.R.C.M., p.s.m., Director of Music Coldstream Guards and the Royal Military School of Music, rearranged the march with additional use of fanfare trumpets under the new title *Knights of the Queen*. This was also included in the Beating of Retreat ceremony by The Household Division on Horse Guards Parade in 1972, and at the Royal Silver Jubilee Pageant held at Wembley Stadium on 30th June 1977 in the presence of the Queen. Here the Mounted Bands and State Trumpeters of the Household Cavalry came into the arena, to join the Massed Bands representing all three Armed Services and already assembled, to a splendid performance of the march played by the entire company of bandsmen totalling over 1400 musicians. Also included in the programme as the fifth item at this Royal Silver Jubilee Pageant was *Bells across the Meadows*, which just a few weeks earlier had been given a rousing performance when it was played as the first item of the Finale of the Beating of Retreat ceremony by The Household Division on Horse Guards Parade - complete with amplified tubular bells!

Ketèlbey's friendship with Paddy Dunn (just 6 days his junior) was in turn to bring a famous military establishment into his life, in the form of the Royal Military School of Music at Kneller Hall, Twickenham. In 1930 Paddy invited the composer to the annual social day and dinner of the Kneller Hall Club, and during the day there were various sporting events laid on, in which members and guests could participate. As Ketèlbey was a keen but not brilliant golfer, his friend Paddy decided to ask a fellow member of the Club, who was also an ex-pupil of the years 1923/4 at the Military School - and who had similar golf credentials to Ketèlbey - to accompany the composer in a game of golf on the Club's 9 hole course. The person in question was a certain Douglas Alexander Pope (1903 - 1984) who at that time was a French horn player in the 2nd Battalion, The Royal Sussex Regiment (later Lieutenant Colonel D.A. Pope, O.B.E., A.R.C.M., Director of Music (1944 - 61) H.M. Coldstream Guards) and his memories of meeting the famous composer, are both interesting and amusing. Upon being introduced to him, Pope immediately noticed what he called "Ketèlbey's 'Pickwickian' appearance" and also his "slight Birmingham accent", and although feeling overawed by having to act as host to the man whose music at that time was scarcely left out of military programmes, he was to feel entirely at ease with him before the first green.

Of the 9 holes of golf played - the longest being 270 yards and the shortest 60 yards - neither played many very good shots, and in this connection the younger man was very impressed by the older's happy outlook on life! The short 60 yard hole involved the amazing task of hitting the ball over the cricket pavilion, when (in Douglas Pope's words) "It would land from a great height in an almost vertical trajectory upon the cricketers or spectators on the other side, but no one ever appears to have been hit!" Ketèlbey managed to clear the pavilion so that he could hole in two, whereas, Pope thought it may have taken himself more like twenty two! After the game Ketèlbey treated his host to a drink in the clubhouse, before the main event dinner in the evening. In conversation with him 'over a pint', Douglas Pope remembered him being very confident but not inclined to talk much about himself, and found him very good company.

Like some of his contemporary composers, Ketèlbey was to be invited to Kneller Hall as a guest tutor/conductor on several occasions during the 1930s, and this association with the School of Music was to become very close to Ketèlbey's heart, whereby in appreciation of it he presented a full score of his Suite *Three Fanciful Etchings* to Captain H. Adkins, the School's Director of Music from 1921 to 1943, on which he inscribed in his own handwriting, "To Capt. H. ADKINS, Mus Bac, With the Compliments of the composer". Ketèlbey fan John Shaw, a retired car worker from Hockley, Birmingham, whose father Leonard was a clarinettist in the Lancashire Fusiliers, and a pupil at Kneller Hall in the mid 1920s, told me how encouraging his late father said it was for himself and fellow pupils when such high profile musicians tutored and conducted them, albeit this was only occasionally. He had vivid memories of Gustav Holst (1874 - 1934) and Kenneth J. Alford and rather vaguer memories of Ketèlbey visiting the Hall in this capacity, whilst he was a pupil there, although I have found no written record of Ketèlbey actually being there as early as this. It is interesting to note that several older people have got Kenneth J. Alford mixed up with Ketèlbey, sometimes believing that this was one of his pseudonyms, and John Shaw said this could well have been the case with his own father.

On a military note it is worth mentioning that by this time Ketèlbey's music had become quite popular in Spain, and that even during the turmoil of the Spanish Civil War, his music was still broadcast there, as in September 1936 when *In a Monastery Garden* was broadcast from Madrid and *Sanctuary of the Heart* from Barcelona.

At about the same time back in England, Ketèlbey had just completed a summer tour of concerts taking in Brighton, Harrogate, Blackpool and Bridlington, and also including a military charity concert in Richmond, Yorkshire, where he conducted the Band of The Green Howards (Alexandra, Princess of Wales' Own Yorkshire Regiment) in a programme of his own works for their Annual Benefit for the Welfare Fund Concert. At these concerts he had introduced his latest composition *With the Roumanian Gypsies - Fantasy*, having earlier in the year introduced it at concerts in Cardiff and Hastings, and at his Annual Kingsway Hall Concert in February.

His friend Paddy Dunn had retired from the Royal Horse Guards in late 1935, and by May 1936 had formed his own orchestra of 25 players from various other London orchestras - mainly the Carl Rosa Opera Company Orchestra. This newly formed orchestra was to play regularly on the Palace Pier, Brighton, from May to October 1936, thus filling a musical void at Brighton which by this time no longer had a municipal orchestra.

This summer season was from the outset to prove an overwhelming success for Paddy Dunn, and in order to add even more impetus to it, he decided to ask his old friend 'Albert the Monk' if he would conduct the orchestra in an 'All Ketèlbey Concert' at the Palace Pier (see plate 47). This was arranged for Sunday evening 2nd August 1936 at 8.00 p.m., and following which a report on the concert appeared in *The Brighton Herald* telling of its success. The full report is reproduced here on pages 107 and 108, as it does I believe give us a comprehensive picture of the composer's typical style and personality, and indeed popularity of such 'All Ketèlbey Concerts', which as we have seen he performed all over the country. A similar but shorter report on the concert which appeared at the same time in the *Brighton Gazette*, went on to say, "On leaving the rostrum he [Ketèlbey] was besieged by autograph hunters and must have signed hundreds before he was at last allowed to leave!"

FAMOUS COMPOSER WITH FAMOUS CONDUCTOR'S BAND

ALBERT KETÈLBEY AT PALACE PIER

Thousands of people who, like the rest of us, had "raved" over "In a Monastery Garden," "Bells Across the Meadow," and other light "classics" by Albert. W. Ketèlbey, had the joy on Sunday night of seeing the world-famous composer in his own agreeable person.

They had the further joy of hearing him conduct an "all-Ketèlbey" programme played by Captain W.J. Dunn's celebrated orchestra in the Palace Pier bandstand.

Captain Dunn conducted the first composition, "With Honour Crowned," a rousing march composed in honour of King George's silver jubilee, and then introduced "my old friend, Albert Ketèlbey," who took over the baton.

Mr. Ketèlbey seemed to infuse the orchestra with his own cheerfulness and vigour, and they played with great spirit. Mr. Ketèlbey's humorous personality and witty asides amused both the audience and the orchestra.

The "Merry Mascots"

The composer gave a brilliant rendering of his composition, "Dance of the Merry Mascots," on the piano, accompanied by the orchestra (conducted by Captain Dunn). Mr. Ketèlbey first told the story of the composition. The mascots go to a fancy dress ball dressed as pierrots, pierrettes, and Japanese and Spanish dancers. They start with a waltz for the pierrots and pierrettes (during which Weber's "Invitation to the dance" is played as a counter melody; then follow two movements for the Japanese and Spanish dancers. The waltz is now resumed, and towards the end some of the mascots who have got a bit too "merry" find it rather difficult to keep time, but they manage to finish altogether! The chimes now indicate that it is near midnight, and the mascots are heard taking their departure.

The piece was applauded enthusiastically, and Mr. Ketèlbey gave an encore of the same piece-as he aptly put it "from where they have had one!"

At the conclusion of the encore, Mr. Ketèlbey asked one of the lady members of the orchestra to take a bouquet to his wife, who was in the audience. A bouquet was also presented to Mrs. Dunn.

The second part of the programme was devoted to special radio favourites from Ketèlbey's works, which of course, included that characteristic composition for which he is world famed, "In a Monastery Garden." Mr. Ketèlbey said that he had been specially asked to play this piece, and that he quite understood that "it would be rather like Christmas without plum pudding" if he did not play it.

Other favourites included such descriptive pieces as "In a Persian Market"-in which members of the orchestra very ably rendered the market gossiping-and, as the composer observed, "they seem to have picked up a good few bargains."

Then came "Sanctuary of the Heart" and "Bells Across the Meadow," and the concert very appropriately concluded with two numbers from the "Cockney Suite" - "Bank Holiday" and "'Appy 'Ampstead."(*sic*)

At the conclusion of the concert Ketèlbey thanked the audience for their very kind reception, and said that the Palace Pier should be congratulated on having such a fine orchestra.

Compositions in 1937 were to include his songs *A Mayfair Cinderella* and *I Dream of all the Worlds*, and on 12th February 1938 back at the Kingsway Hall, Ketèlbey conducted on this occasion the City of Portsmouth Orchestra in a concert of his works, in which he was assisted by Lieutenant Vivian Dunn. At this concert was the first performance of two new compositions, including a piano novelty called *Sunbeams and Butterflies*, which at the time was reported as having been written just a few days earlier, with the interesting anecdote, that whilst pondering for a suitable title for the piece, his wife Charlotte made the comments, "It's a lovely day today, Albert, full of sunshine and butterflies". This of course seems a strange thing to say in February, and it may perhaps have been said earlier in either 1924 when he had written *Schmetterling* or in 1926 when he had written *Butterfly's Frolic*, from which this *Sunbeams and Butterflies* had been reworked as a final version. The other new work, which became quite popular, was a suite in three movements entitled *In Holiday Mood*, the three movements being; (1) *On the Promenade*, (2) *Down the Stream*, (3) *The Illuminated Fête*.

The concerts continued throughout the remainder of the 1930s and the *Musical Opinion* issue for May 1939 reported that ".....A Ketèlbey night means "house full", for the "King of Light Music" is exceedingly popular with orchestras and audiences alike....". Following a concert at the Bath Spring Musical Festival, the *Bath Weekly Chronicle and Herald* reported that "Albert Ketèlbey is the most popular figure in the world of light music today", and shortly after this he conducted a programme of his works at a Festival Concert at the Winter Gardens Pavilion, Weston-super-Mare. This was on the evening of Easter Sunday 1939, with the Municipal Orchestra, whose resident conductor was now Mozart Allan - an old friend and colleague of Harold Ketèlbey, having earlier been principal cello in Lyell-Tayler's Brighton Orchestra, in which Harold was at the time leader.

Reproduced on pages 110 and 111 is an extract from the Souvenir
Programme for this concert, showing the compositions which were
included. Interestingly item 12 on the programme, billed as a *Romance*
turned out to be Ketèlbey's prize work *The Phantom Melody*, which Mozart
Allan played, accompanied at the piano by the composer, and at the close of
the concert both were reported as receiving an extraordinary ovation. The
following day Mr. and Mrs. Ketèlbey were entertained to lunch at the Grand
Atlantic Hotel by the Mayor of Weston, where upon leaving Ketèlbey said,
"I am taking with me memories of a very enjoyable visit to Weston-super
Mare".

PROGRAMME

SPECIAL AND EXCLUSIVE VISIT OF
THE WORLD-FAMOUS COMPOSER-CONDUCTOR

ALBERT KETELBEY

(" The King of Light Music "—Decca Record Co.'s advertisement)
who will personally direct the following programme of his popular works.

SUPPORTED BY

THE MUNICIPAL ORCHESTRA
THE WESTON-SUPER-MARE GLEE PARTY

AND

Solo Violoncello, MOZART ALLAN.

1. March—" Knights of the King " (assisted by the Weston Glee Party)

2. Gypsy Overture—" Chal Romano "
   Andante Pesante.   Allegro Scherzando.   Andante quasi recitative.
   Presto.

3. Dance Intermezzo—" Wedgwood Blue "

4. Fantasy—" With the Roumanian Gypsies "
   A Romany melody.   Characteristic Tzigane movement.   Shepherd's Pie.   The Song of the Romany-Gypsy Dance.

5. Meditation—" Sanctuary of the Heart " (by special request)
   (assisted by the Weston Glee Party.   Soloist—William Nettle)

6. Descriptive—" By the blue Hawaiin Waters "
   Introduction.   " Hula " Dance.   " Kanaka " lover's call.   Song of the " Hula " Girls.   Dance of the Betrothal Ceremony.

7. Intermezzo—" Bells across the Meadows "

8. A Dream Picture—" In a Camp of the Ancient Britons "
   (Specially composed after a visit to Worlebury Camp)
   This piece portrays the dream of a visitor who in imagination revisits the historic site in its ancient setting.   Visions of Druids, Ancient Britons, Roman Invaders and the ensuing battle pass before him in this dream.   He is awakened by a waltz being played by a band near by, the waltz gradually evolving from the melody of the Invocation.

Page 1 of programme of music for Weston-super-Mare concert.
Easter Sunday 1939.

9. Piano and Orchestra—" Dance of the Merry Mascots "

> The Composer at the Piano. Conducted by Mozart Allan.
>
> The mascots go to a fancy dress ball, as pierrots, Japanese and Spanish dancers. They start with a waltz for the pierrots (during which Weber's " Invitation to the Waltz " is played as a counter-melody) then follow two movements for the Japanese and Spanish dancers ; the waltz is now resumed, and towards the end some of the mascots who have got a bit *too* merry, find it rather difficult to keep in time ; the chimes now indicate that it is near midnight and the mascots are heard taking their departure.

INTERVAL

10. Suite—" In Holiday Mood "

> (1) On the Promenade
>
> (2) Down the Stream
>
> (3) The Illuminated Fete

11. The famous Intermezzo—" In a Monastery Garden "

> (assisted by the Weston Glee Party)

12. VIOLONCELLO SOLO—" Romance "

> MOZART ALLAN
>
> (accompanied at the Piano by the Composer)

13. Oriental Fantasy—" In a Chinese Temple Garden "

> (assisted by the Weston Glee Party)

14. Cockney Suite—" Cameos of London Life "

> (1) State Procession (Buckingham Palace)
>
> (2) Cockney Lover (Lambeth Walk)
>
> > This number portrays a *sentimental* aspect of the Lambeth Walk, and was composed several years before the present dance tune of the same title. It is founded on the street whistle, " Arf a pint of mild and bitter."
>
> (3) Elegy (The Cenotaph)
>
> (4) Bank Holiday ('Appy 'Ampstead ")

" GOD SAVE THE KING "

Page 2 of programme of music for Weston-super-Mare concert.
Easter Sunday 1939.

CHAPTER 10

TIMES OF SADNESS

......If faithful to my trust I stay,
No fate can fill me with dismay,
Love holds the key to set me free,
And love will find a way..........

Harry Graham/Harold Fraser-Simson.

*A*s late as November 1940 Ketèlbey made recordings with his own
Concert Orchestra of some of his most popular compositions on the
Decca record label, which were issued on a set of five ten-inch records,
and following which he was invited by Mr. Leslie A. Perowne of the BBC
to Broadcasting House to be interviewed about these. Like Ketèlbey, Leslie
Perowne was a 'Brummie' by birth and had grown to have much admiration
for the composer's music, and yet ironically it was he, you may recall from
Chapter 6, who later issued that famous edict banning *Bells across the
Meadows* from being broadcast by the BBC during the war. Perowne
worked on the programme side of the BBC, and had met Ketèlbey in this
respect on several occasions, having himself first broadcast a programme of
Ketèlbey's music on the National Wave on Sunday 27th March 1938, which
he called "KETÈLBEY, Master of Melody". Just as Albert was as popular
as ever over the air waves, so it would appear, Lottie was as over-protective
as ever towards him, as borne out by Leslie Perowne. Having accepted his
invitation to Broadcasting House for this interview in 1940, Albert decided
to take Lottie along with him, and of meeting the composer again and Lottie
for the first time, Perowne said, "He was a gentle, white -haired old boy who
brought his rather tiresome wife with him. I wanted to interview him but
she would insist on interrupting every time I asked Ketèlbey a question and
tried to answer for him. I could have hit her!"

Although concerts were now of course restricted due to the war effort, at
concerts in Southport and Cheltenham in July and August 1942 he was
reported to be very informal with his audiences, who still delighted in his
music. A Kingsway Hall concert held on the afternoon of 13th February

1943, was reported to have drawn a crowded audience, at which "conspicuously outstanding" was a new marching song *Fighting for Freedom*, which had recently been performed and broadcast for the first time by the orchestra of H.M. Royal Marines (Portsmouth Division) under Captain Vivian Dunn, and sung by Robert Layton. The composer had written this song in response to Winston Churchill's famous speech, wherein he had said, "We shall fight on the beaches, we shall fight on the landing grounds, we shall fight in the fields and in the streets, we shall fight in the hills, we shall never surrender". As in previous times of war, such as the Boer War, when he wrote the song *There's something in the English after all* (with words by Florence Hoare); the First World War, when he wrote *The trumpet-voice of Motherland is calling*; so in this the Second World War his patriotism came to the fore in writing this piece, and it speaks volumes of the character and patriotism of the man that during the war, when in his sixties, he gave his services to his country in fulfilling the role of a special constable at every opportune moment.

The effect of war, however, changes many, many things. So it was that following the Second World War tastes in music began to change, and had probably begun so to do during the war itself. The music of the composer thus began to loose its popularity, and the once popular 'Ketèlbey' concerts did not immediately resume. This decline in popularity coupled with the possible effect the war had on the man himself is perhaps why his power of composition began to wane and lose novelty, and why in reality little else of any real significance was composed by him, and the reason why he has often been referred to as being spiritually of the pre-Second World War years. Some have said that his power of original composition actually began to wane after 1930, and there is certainly some truth in this when one bears in mind that those popular compositions which have endured were, with the exception of a handful of other pieces, composed in his most prolific era from 1912 to 1930.

Having said this, he was still keen to carry on composing and a continuing professionalism in his approach, is witnessed by a letter dated 23rd February 1945 (see page 115) to Mr. Harry Mortimer O.B.E. (1902-1992) a highly respected figure in the world of brass bands, concerning an overture he had then written for brass band. This he worked through with Mr. Mortimer and became his *Overture - The Adventurers* which was first performed and broadcast by the Fairy Aviation Works Band under Harry Mortimer on 18th November 1945. This was later worked into an orchestral piece but was not noted as one of his best compositions. In 1947 he wrote a piano novelty with orchestral accompaniment entitled *Skitty Kitty* which was published under a new pseudonym, Dennis Charlton, but much more successful in the same year was his flamboyant *Caprice Pianistique* for piano and orchestra.

Feb.23/45

Dear Mr. Mortimer,

I have now completed the new overture I have composed specially for Brass Band. I have written out a Piano Conductor part but before scoring the Band parts I should like you to look at it & tell me frankly if you think it is good enough for the Standard you are aiming at in the Brass Band world. I would prefer to leave it personally at your BBC office instead of trusting to the post, if you would let me know your best time for me to call. (Any morning about 11.30 would suit me best.)

With kind regards.

Yours sincerely,

Albert W. Ketèlbey

Albert W. Ketèlbey
Composer and Conductor

15 LINDFIELD GARDENS, HAMPSTEAD, N.W.3   HAMPSTEAD 2066

Feb 23/45

Dear Mr Mortimer

I have now completed the new overture I have composed specially for Brass Band. I have written out a Piano Cond^r part but before scoring the Band parts I should like you to look at it & tell me frankly if you think it is good enough for the standard you are aiming at in the Brass Band world. I would prefer to leave it personally at your BBC Off. instead of trusting to the post, if you would let me know your best time for me to call. (any morning about 11.30 would suit me best.) With kind regards

Yours Sincerely

Albert W Ketèlbey

These things apart, he was now content to let the world go by and appreciate the simple joys of life - the company of a loving wife at his welcoming home where he could sit at his favourite Victorian desk and work on his music, and where he could relax and play his favourite billiards game - not realising that so soon after the war other events were to unfold and devastate his simple contentment. These began during the bitter winter of 1946 - 47, when one night the couple's cherished Hampstead home was flooded when the rising main to their home, frozen by the sub-zero temperatures, suddenly burst at the seams. He and Lottie tried desperately to salvage his library of books, manuscripts, scores, cine films and private papers, but most of these were lost in the quagmire conditions. As a consequence of working in the damp and cold conditions in this salvage attempt, both of them soon became seriously ill with pneumonia and were rushed into Regents Park Nursing Home, where tragically just two days later on 20th February 1947 his beloved Lottie, with whom he had not long before celebrated their Ruby Wedding Anniversary, died aged 75. Albert, now aged 71, got over his own pneumonia, but the loss of Lottie left him devastated and truly heartbroken. Without children of their own, understandably, the couple had over the years become increasingly devoted to each other, the extent of which must have intensified his sorrow. This in turn led the now lonely old gentleman, whose joyful music had brought such happiness to others, to suffer depression and for a short time a nervous breakdown.

Although family and friends had offered to help him, he appeared to spurn their genuine love and concern, and in his low state he decided to sell his Hampstead home which had meant so much to him and Lottie, and move into a hotel. He did, however, consent to his favourite nephew Louis Lewis and his wife Dorothy helping him in the daunting task of disposing of the house and contents. His London base then became Hendon Hall Hotel (see plate 38) at Ashley Lane, Hendon, North London. Whilst here he was attended by a Doctor Gordon Wells who lived opposite the hotel, who got to know him very well, and maybe it was he who prompted his patient to take a convalescence break, for in an effort to recuperate, for a time he stayed at several hotels on the south coast.

It was during this time, in the summer of 1947, that whilst on holiday with his family in Folkestone, Ken Hinton from Birmingham noticed that a band was playing on the bandstand of the Green on Leas Cliff, and so took advantage of some spare deck chairs and sat down to enjoy the remainder of the concert. Ken discovered that it was the Gold Coast Police Band from Africa who were playing, and after listening to a few pieces, he then noticed the conductor offer his baton to a gentleman sitting on the front row, who duly refused.

The conductor then returned to his rostrum and conducted the band himself in a performance of *In a Monastery Garden*, which made Ken rather intrigued as to who the mystery man in the front row was. At the end of the concert he therefore wasted no time in making his way to the front to discover that it was none other than Albert W. Ketèlbey. Ken, who himself played the accordion, then had an interesting chat with the maestro about his music, and although it was only months since the trauma of his wife's death, Ketèlbey had not lost his good sense of humour, which brought a chuckle to Ken after he had told the composer of one of his own musical exploits whilst in the forces, as follows:-

> At Christmastime in 1945, Ken who was then a crash tender in 91 Spitfire Squadron of the RAF, was on service in Rangoon, and was asked if he would perform on his accordion with one of his comrades who was a violinist, on the local radio. He told Ketèlbey that they agreed to this, and that one piece which they performed was his own *In a Monastery Garden*, to which Mr. K replied, "In that case you owe me a few bob in royalties!" He duly gave Ken his autograph on the back of a band-card, bade him good-bye and with his lady companion (probably his youngest sister Doris) on his arm, walked away unrecognised by the summer crowd, into Folkestone town.

During this stay in Folkestone, Ketèlbey was one day walking along the sea front, when the pianist Jack Byfield, who was in the town playing with Albert Sandler, met him. Jack Byfield, who with the cellist Reginald Kilbey often played Ketèlbey's *Phantom Melody*, later commented on this chance meeting saying that in chatting with the composer he deduced that he was still struggling to get over the loss of his wife, which he said was "a terrible blow" to him. He referred to Ketèlbey as "a very kind and gentle man" who he "liked very much", who told him that he was planning to visit his brother Harold in South Africa. However, other events and particularly new romance (of which I will elaborate later) meant that this plan would not come to fruition.

Also in this same glorious summer of 1947, and believed to be during this same stay of Ketèlbey's at Folkestone, Lieutenant Colonel Douglas A. Pope, who was now Musical Director of H.M. Coldstream Guards also met him again. This was on Sunday 20th July 1947 whilst Pope was conducting his band in a military concert on Leas Cliff Green, he noticed Ketèlbey in the audience. Not thinking that it would be the done thing for him to ask the composer to conduct the band in one of his compositions, instead he duly acknowledged his presence in the audience, and asked him if he would like the band to play one of his pieces. To this Ketèlbey replied, "Well, that's your choice", and Pope decided that as it was a Sunday, he would conduct them in *In a Monastery Garden*, followed by *Bells across the Meadows*.

At the end of the concert Ketèlbey thanked Pope and invited him for an early evening drink, which Pope duly accepted, and so met up with him later that day at the Baytree Bar. After one or two "Dog'd Noses"[21], Ketèlbey, who Pope also said was still feeling the loss of his wife greatly, opened up a little in his conversation with him. He was naturally reluctant to talk about Lottie, but said that this present stay at Folkestone was in response to an invitation to stay at the Metropole Hotel, from the manager there who was an old friend, and who had given him an open invitation to go there following Lottie's death. He talked very little about his own achievements, but they did talk particularly about the popularity of *'Appy 'Ampsted* from his *Cockney Suite*, and he complimented Pope for the great care he took with the "Bank Holiday noises", whenever his band performed it. He was very pleased as to how well his music had been received abroad, although he did show some tinge of regret that his more serious aspirations were not appreciated by the public at large, whilst at the same time accepting the fact that his name had become associated with memorable tunes.

From this conversation Pope was left with the impression that he had not done much composing latterly, but he did tell him that his publisher Bosworth's were wanting a military band version of a piece he had composed entitled *Birthday of the Little Princess*. He then asked Pope if he could do this arranging, which he agreed to do but unfortunately, later, due to problems of flexibility in transcription he had to give up. In speaking of other composers, and particularly Haydn Wood (1882 - 1959), he told Pope that at one stage when living in Hampstead they were close neighbours with adjoining gardens, and that in the summer - with windows open - they could overhear each other playing the piano. He then amused Pope, when with that hallmark twinkle in his eye, he said that this could lead them to suspect each other of plagiarism! There may well be some real truth in this, for as far as I know the two composers never did befriend each other.

The "homebird" man that he was meant that in reality living in hotels did not really suit Ketèlbey, but still, the sea air and convalescence break which he had taken must have done him good. This is borne out in a letter dated

---

21 A "Dog'd Nose" is half a pint of beer with some gin in it.

2nd October 1947 to the BBC, shown on page 120 which speaks volumes of the resolution of the man at 72 years of age, and gives us a small and rare insight into his heart at this time.

It was possibly when he was further convalescing, staying at the Royal Exeter Hotel in Bournemouth, that he was to meet the lady who was to become his second wife. Whilst here he must have been missing his music somewhat, because he decided to ask the manageress if he could have permission to put a piano in his room, which she duly declined to give, being concerned that his playing may disturb other hotel guests. Still not inclined to give up easily, he presented his argument to justify his request and apparently things got a 'little heated'. She did not succumb to his request for the piano, however, but she did later succumb to his charm, for from their initial fiery encounter there developed a romance and courtship. Maybe this was the reason why he had "a merry twinkle behind his rimless glasses and hummed and sang as he conducted some of his bright and beautiful melodies on St. Anne's-on-the-Sea Pier, on the night of 1st September 1948" - as so reported by the *Blackpool Evening Gazette* the following day. At this packed concert at the pier's Floral Hall, the resident conductor of the Pier Orchestra, Mr. Lionel Johns, after taking the first part of the programme, then introduced the composer to the audience to take the second part. Ketèlbey conducted several of his well-known pieces, and during one of his popular chats with the audience he told them that he was now suffering from neuritis in his hands, and to their delight then glibly played the piano for his *Dance of the Merry Mascots*.

He left St. Anne's as a happy man saying, "It has been worth coming all the way from London for the orchestra played beautifully", and within two months had vacated his room at Hendon Hall Hotel in London to marry the new lady in his life. On 30th October 1948 the 45-year-old Mrs. Mabel Maud Pritchett became his wife at a ceremony at Bournemouth Register Office, at which the two main signature witnesses were his youngest sister Doris (thought to be the only close relative present at the wedding) and his old friend and "agent" Tommy Kottaun.

Hendon Hall Hotel N.W.4   2nd October 1947
                                           Ref. 03/M/HD

Dear Mr. Danse,

Re yours of the 9th July.

It has remained unanswered before this, because I have, firstly, been away for 2 months for my health, and, secondly because I have been since my return occupied with preparations and rehearsals for my first "Ketèlbey" concert since 1944, so I had a lot to do.

My concert was at Worthing with Herbert Lodge's orchestra and choir, - it was in the nature of a "come-back" after the sorrows of my wife's death after 2 days illness which I feared had put me permanently out of action, however, I braced myself for the ordeal and it turned out a big success.

Now about my suggestion of "Composers' own Favourites" I feel that such a feature might be of interest to listeners as an indication of what the composer prefers out of his own works, though they probably will not be the "popular" ones. I have sketched out a programme of about 40 minutes for orchestra and Soprano Vocalist which I enclose. I believe Miss Perilli has sung successfully for the BBC, - she was extremely attractive in the two songs I have given. I shall be interested to know the views of Mr. Lawrence on my proposition and shall be happy to meet him any time to discuss it.

> With kind regards.
> Yours sincerely,

> Albert W. Ketèlbey

Composers' own Favourites
KETÈLBEY
Gypsy Overture "Chal Romano"
Suite "In a Fairy Realm"
2 Songs (a) King Cupid
           (b) Mayfair Cinderella
(accompanied at piano)   Miss Maria Perilli
          Two Serious pieces
          (a) A passing stormcloud on a Summer's Day
          (b) Elegy from Cockney Suite
          "Illuminated Fete"
          (from Suite "In Holiday Mood")

Conducted by Composer or otherwise as desired by the Programme Director.

CHAPTER 11

ROOKSTONE AND *MUSIC FOR YOU*

That best portion of a good man's life, his little, nameless,
unremembered acts of kindness and love.

William Wordsworth.

*T*he new Mrs. Ketèlbey was previously the widow of a Mr. Cecil Pritchett
with whom she had lived at Newport on the Isle of Wight, and her father
William John Hebdige was prior to his retirement Chief Prison Officer at
Parkhurst Prison on the Island. She was good for Ketèlbey, being very
much down-to-earth and a good-natured person, who had a high regard for
the late Lottie - whose mantle role of protecting Albert she soon took up,
even promising "Ket" that in her lifetime nothing should be allowed to bother
him. It was perhaps her love of the peace and beauty of the Isle of Wight,
which had led them to decide to settle down in retirement there, and
according to his Isle of Wight bank manager Mr. F. R. Willis, Albert and
Mabel lived initially at Harbour Mount, Kings Road, Bembridge, and I
reproduce on page 122 an interesting letter from Mr. Willis to William Neve
which briefly explains the friendship which ensued between the bank
manager and his famous customer.

Their home in Bembridge was only a temporary residence, for within
months of their marriage they had purchased "Rookstone" bungalow (see
plate 50) on Egypt Hill in West Cowes, which was to become another
beloved haven for the "homebird" and his new wife (where he was able to
have his "Grand" piano without worry of upsetting those infamous hotel
guests!) and where he was to remain for most of the rest of his life. It seems
ironical (some may say providential) that having written so many authentic
pieces of music relating to the East and the Orient, and particularly *In the*
Mystic Land of Egypt, and bearing in mind that in all of his travels abroad,
not once did he visit the East or the Orient, that perchance he should finish
up living in a road bearing such a name! The origin of this road being called
Egypt Hill goes back to the year 1771, when the peninsula now called Egypt
Point near to where Egypt Hill is located, was first recorded as Egypt Cliff.

Telephone: Chillerton 209

Knowle
Chillerton, Newport
Isle of Wight.

14th March 1975

Dear Sir,

Albert Ketèlbey
of Harbour Mount
Bembridge IW.

I retired many years ago from management of Lloyds Bank Newport. One day a gentleman came to see me to open an account. Having taken a specimen signature etc. & chatting of the ordinary things of the day he left - it was then I realised who he was & chased after him in the High St. with the words that I did not think I was in the presence of so great a man. He was deeply touched & we became friends - he would often call in for a chat when in Newport. One day he was most upset - a wasp had stung him in the "webbing" between the fingers & he no longer could as he said "stretch the octave". Later he told me he had written another piece & it was to be played over the radio, after which he asked did I hear it. "Yes I did" - "What did it convey to you?" - (Now, sir, I have no music knowledge nor can I read music, but Albert always said I got more out of music than he - for I was deeply moved & he listened for mistakes!!) However, I told him it gave me the impression of rolling countryside & hills - right he said I will call it "On Brading Down". So I countered & said may I have a copy when published - and autographed? Alas I do not think it was published for he died.

He was from my brief association a charming little man (I am in the 6' 0" very much plus). I apologise for my writing but A.D. does not help!

Yours truly.

F. R. Willis.

Prior to this date the area was simply known as West Cliff - from its situation west of Cowes, but took the new name from "Egypt House" a large mansion built between 1769 and 1775, set in gardens at the base of Egypt Hill. The house was so named because the area which it was to occupy had earlier been inhabited by a band of gypsies, and one interesting historical note concerns a Miss Clementine Hozier. She was a guest here when attending Cowes Week in 1908, and whilst in residence was invited by a certain Winston Spencer Churchill (later Sir Winston) to Blenheim Palace, where shortly after arriving he made his formal proposal of marriage. Similarly, it seems ironical to me that with his writing of music of the Orient, but also bearing in mind that musical input he had earlier made into the world of the silent movies, that on 4th August 1930 had been opened at 32/40 High Street, Aston, Birmingham - about 300 yards from where he was born - a cinema called "The Orient", which was designed and ornamented throughout in Eastern style.

Now quite portly, his hair turned snow white and parted on the side instead of the middle he would often wear his favourite black Homburg hat, which meant that in appearance he looked very distinguished. Life in the main was now one of retirement and the enjoyment of the simplicities of a quiet life at his bungalow with its surroundings overlooking the Solent. His sister Doris, commenting on her brother's demeanour, once said, "He always conveyed a sense of power, and certainly in later life when he put on weight, had an authoritive presence which was unmistakeable. If he went into a restaurant, I assure you all the waiters came smartly to attention, and of course he never dealt with anyone but the Maitre D'Hotel. I found it often embarrassing, but he was completely unselfconscious, entirely absorbed in what he had in hand at the moment". The couple's intention now was to maintain privacy - even to the point of having erected a high fence around "Rookstone" bungalow, which was really out of character to its style and location. Whilst he would welcome visits from people interested in his music, such as the musician Arthur Cole then conductor of Cheltenham Spa Orchestra, and his bass player Bob Thompson, who he warmly welcomed to "Rookstone" in 1950, he did not want any bother with reporters.

He did not really get involved in local musical activities on the Island, but I have discovered some small aspects of his enjoyment of the local music scene. He would occasionally go to Ryde and listen to the Ryde Municipal Orchestra, being spotted by the orchestra's percussionist Kenneth Watkinson whenever he was in the audience. At one concert in 1950, after hearing them play some of his pieces, Ketèlbey sent a message to Henry W. Jolliffe, the conductor, complimenting him on the orchestra's performance of these, also saying how grateful he was that his works were being featured by the orchestra, and suggesting that when he had the time he would like him to join himself and Mabel for tea at "Rookstone". Unfortunately Henry Jolliffe never did take up this invitation, and when William Neve visited him on the Isle of Wight in October 1974, he spoke of his sadness in not going to "Rookstone" for tea, but also of his gladness when as conductor of the orchestra, he received constant requests for the works of Ketèlbey, and especially *Bells across the Meadows*, when he had the aforementioned Kenneth Watkinson as his popular percussionist - whom he said was a very good player of those "famous tubular bells". Likewise he enjoyed listening to the local Cowes Town Band, and at one stage kindly presented them with a new set of drums. Jack Jones, then the curator of Carisbrooke Castle on the Island, also recalled how on one occasion Ketèlbey visited the castle with some friends. He remarked how spritely the composer was for his age, and said that his main memory was that of him delightfully trying his hand on the Positif organ, once played by the daughter of Charles I when she was resident in Carisbrooke Castle in the seventeenth century, and said to be one of the oldest organs in the country.

He was also to meet again his friend Douglas A. Pope, whilst living on the Island. This was when Pope visited the Island with the Band of the Coldstream Guards to perform a series of concerts, and at one evening concert Ketèlbey went along to see his old friend and hear the band play, taking the applause when his march *Knights of the King* was played. After the concert the two men met again, and he told Pope that he had been unhappy living in hotels, so had married again for companionship, and upon meeting the new Mrs. Ketèlbey, Pope said to her "Take good care of him, he's part of us". Lieutenant Colonel Douglas A. Pope, O.B.E. is remembered today as a brilliant military musician, and commenting once on his friend's music said "I compare 'Ketèlbey's ear-ticklers' to 'Beecham's lollipops'". He also referred to Ketèlbey's wide spread popularity long before radio, the sincerity of his compositions, and his sharper powers of description than other composers. In speaking of his inherent kindness, he said he would receive a letter every Christmas from the composer, besides a card and some of his favourite *Passing Cloud* cigarettes.

Mabel must have taken heed of Douglas Pope's words to her, for it was soon evident that he had again found happiness with his new wife and companion, and mellowed well in his new surroundings, even to the point where he would accompany Mabel on her regular shopping trips to Newport and other towns on the Island. It is believed that by now he had given up driving, for his regular taxi driver on these outings was Wilfred Dorrington, and on the first occasion that he drove them he was asked rather imperiously by

Mr. Ketèlbey to follow Mrs. Ketèlbey to the shops so that he could carry her shopping for her, whilst he waited in the car. However, the down-to-earth Mabel would have none of this, and so the norm became that he too would wait in the car with her husband whilst she shopped and did her own carrying! So it was that on several occasions Wilfred would sit waiting with his famous client, and by asking him a leading question would get him talking about himself and his career, until Mabel returned.

On a few occasions the composer was to come out of retirement and back into public view, when he would pick up his baton to conduct performances of his music to audiences who by now tended to be of the older generation. At these his hospitality and pleasure in being first at the bar after the concert, to order those drinks for his performers, were apparently still as great as ever! He could not, however, extend the slightest generosity towards the BBC, when he felt the need to write to them in 1949.

Although light music was not now as popular as it had once been, it was none the less still a popular form of music in the post war years and still very prominent on the radio air waves of the BBC. The fact that the BBC began to neglect his music after the war saddened him much, and had adverse effects on his income from performing rights, which began to decline dramatically, and when in 1949 they broadcast a 'Festival of Light Music' without a single one of his compositions, he was hurt deeply to the point of bitterness, whereby in a curt letter dated 24th March 1949 to Sir William Haley at the BBC, he called the omission "a public insult". He had the right to feel justified in making this statement, and deserves some sympathy, when one bears in mind the literally thousands of broadcasts made of his music up to the war years.

At 74 years of age he really had no need to "burn any more bridges", and so could it have been that once again that part of his character was riled, as it was in the past by those merciless critics, which led him to write in such a vein? In any case, maybe his short "to the point" original letter was sufficient to soothe his anger, for as far as is known he did not bother to "bite back" when in the scathing response to his letter, from the BBC, he was told (amongst other things) that ".....their choice was made on musical grounds only!.....".

I wonder, could it have been in further appeasing his anger to this rebuff that led him to revert to his serious mode once more, and write his appropriately named, and beautiful piano piece, *Angelo d'amore* - Angel of Love? In the same year he also wrote his song *My Star of Love*.

Some say that his outcry of anger with the BBC "sealed his fate" with them, and further adversely effected the future broadcasting of his music. If this was true, in reality it was only one contributing factor in a general

"Rookstone" Egypt Hill
Cowes I.W.

March 24/49

Dear ~~Sir~~,

I consider the complete omission of my music from the Light Music Festival is a public insult by the B.B.C. & requires an explanation.

Yours Truly,

Albert W. Ketèlbey

Sir William Haley

Registered Post

Albert W. Ketèlbey
Composer and Conductor

~~42 LONDON GARDENS, HAMPSTEAD, N.W.3~~

"Rookstone", Egypt Hill, H.
Cowes I.W.

March 24/49

Dear Sir

I consider the complete omission of any music from the Light music Festival is a public insult by the B.B.C. & requires an explanation.

Yours truly,

Albert W. Ketèlbey

Sir William Haley

demise of light music into the 1960s. In any event it did not stop them occasionally broadcasting concerts of his music into the 1950s, as on 21st July 1950 when the first performance of his composition *Italian Twilight* was broadcast, and also on 13th July 1951 when they broadcast a "Special Ketèlbey Concert" performed at Worthing by Herbert Lodge and the Worthing Municipal Orchestra.

There were also a few more happy concert appearances in store for him, as in 1950 he was reported as looking a lot younger than his 75 years, when he conducted a concert of his works with Arthur Cole's Spa Orchestra, at Cheltenham. Two other happy appearances in the public eye came when he appeared on television. In the late 1950s he was interviewed by Barry Westwood for local Southern Television, but earlier in 1953 he was interviewed by the very popular musician of the 1940s and 50s, Eric Robinson (1908 - 1974), who for many years with his own orchestra presented the very successful *Music for You* programme on BBC television.

In the early summer months of 1953 Eric Robinson was apparently reviewing the success of his television programme, and in looking to the future and its continued success, eventually determined to strike a happy medium between the familiar and the new. This guise and a chance remark by one of the members of his orchestra asking if Ketèlbey was still alive, gave birth to the idea of inviting the composer to appear on *Music for You*.

So it was that he went to see the composer - who he humorously referred to as a young man of seventy eight - at his "Rookstone" home. Whilst he was kindly received by Ketèlbey, he did take some convincing about the desire of his appearing before the cameras. This reluctance, Robinson later said, was not because Ketèlbey felt too old to make the journey to London or because he had any doubts about the quality of the programme. It was he said because of the composer's "simple unaffected modesty", which led him to believe that no one at this late stage of his life would be interested in seeing him on television. Through Eric Robinson's kind persuasion the composer eventually agreed to appear on the programme on the evening of Wednesday 5th August 1953. When Eric Robinson told him that he intended to screen a film of a monastery garden on the programme, whilst his famous piece was being played, his insistent modesty again brought the answer, "That will be a lot nicer to look at than to hear my music".

When the programme was broadcast the spontaneous wit of Ketèlbey amused Eric Robinson and delighted viewers, when in interview the presenter asked him "Are you still composing?", he answered, "Well, I'm certainly not de-composing!"

One of the last people from the musical world to visit him at his Isle of Wight home was the biographer and writer Peter Gammond - one of this country's leading authorities on popular music and the author of the extensive *Oxford Companion to Popular Music*. He went along with a photographer to see him, and having taken some photographs, which Ketèlbey duly autographed, Peter Gammond joined him for tea which was served on the lawn at his home. He recalls that Ketèlbey was by then a decidedly stout, white-haired old gentleman with gold-rimmed glasses, who was at the time apparently enjoying playing regular games of chess with some local enthusiasts. Whilst he could not get him to talk much about himself or his works, he was happy to reminisce about those old days of working in theatre, ranging from pantomime to Charlot Revues and working with Gertie Millar at the Vaudeville, besides those stars he worked with at Columbia, lavishing praise on these and other old colleagues and fellow composers.

CHAPTER 12

ENDURANCE

Patience is a bitter plant but it bears sweet fruit.

German Proverb.

*A*fter some ten happy years spent together at "Rookstone" and after writing what was to be his last composition - *The Swiss Dancing Doll*, Albert and Mabel decided to leave their beloved bungalow on the steep slope of Egypt Hill, and move to a luxury private apartment 41 Osborne Court,on the flat seafront Parade of West Cowes (see plate 51), and it was here on the night of 26th November 1959 that the old gentleman passed away at the age of 84 due to renal and heart failure. Alas, his thought of composing another international hit like *In a Monastery Garden* which he had 'matter of factly' shared with Peter Gammond during his interview, or his writing something about himself and his works, which he had with "kindly reluctance" promised Peter he would do, were sadly never to be. His passing received scant attention in the annals of the obituary press, and it is a deplorable fact that just eight people attended his funeral on 1st December 1959 at Golders Green Crematorium, North London. The man who had known such fame was thus temporarily - even coldly - forgotten, but the warmth of his music was destined to live on, and after the death of its creator even attain, at least in some measure, that "classical" recognition he had so vehemently inwardly desired throughout his life. I say this, not merely being my opinion, but in observing certain facts, the sum total of which is the latent opinion of others:-

(1) Performing right earnings have continued to achieve growth since 1959, making steady progress until 1970 and more significant progress until 1985 (the last year for which figures were published) as shown in the following table:-

A. W. Ketèlbey Performing Right Earnings [22]

Year	£	% increase on previous year quoted
1960	3,168	
1965	5,221	64.80
1970	5,269	0.92
1975	7,470	41.77
1980	12,061	61.46
1985	21,079	74.77

(2) In 1991, with much co-operation from the composer Ernest Tomlinson and the Light Music Society's Library of Light-Orchestral Music, HNH International Ltd. of Hong Kong began issuing an excellent new series of orchestral recordings on compact disc on their 'Marco Polo' label, under the heading British Light Music. In this series, which was very much the brain-child of the New Zealand music producer and artistic director Murray Khouri, they have embraced a wide selection of the music of British composers under this genre, including Eric Coates, Edward German, Archibald Joyce, Haydn Wood and many others. In 1992 a recording was made of the music of Ketèlbey (8.223442) and in 1998 under the auspices of my research work I made contact with HNH International Ltd. in Hong Kong and their United Kingdom distributors Select Music and Video Distribution Ltd. of Redhill, Surrey, to try to establish how this compact disc of Ketèlbey's music under the series had fared. Their help and encouragement in this aspect - and indeed my wider work - was first class, and I was thrilled to discover that the Ketèlbey recording has been one of the most successful of the series, with total world sales then topping 7,000 and still growing, of which 5,000 covered Europe including approximately 1,500 into the United Kingdom, some 1,000 North America and Canada, and the remainder mainly Australia and Japan. From the titles of several of Ketèlbey's works and their oriental accent, it is probably not surprising that his music is still quite popular in Japan. In this respect I was very interested

[22] Source: *Harmonious Alliance - A History of the Performing Right Society.* Cyril Ehrlich. Pub. Oxford University Press 1989.

to learn from the organist and choir master Michael Potter of St. John's Church, Wimbledon, during a visit I made there in October 1997, that some five years earlier a Japanese producer with cameraman and crew had visited and filmed the church as part of a programme on Ketèlbey, which they were making for Japanese Television, as part of a series of programmes on British composers of classical music.

What I was also very interested to learn from HNH International Ltd., was the fact that a double compact disc issue in 1995 under their 'Marco Polo' label (8.223699 and 8.223700) of some 45 piano works of Ketèlbey, including several of his romantic pieces, and brilliantly played by the Australian pianist Rosemary Tuck, had also fared very well, with total world sales by then in the region of 3,500, with regional sales patterns being very similar to that of his orchestral works.

(3) Some music writers say that British light music now comes under the edict of "Easy Listening". I find it interesting, however, that when I visit the large and famous record stores - H.M.V., Virgin, Tower, Dillons, W.H. Smith, etc., I do indeed find the music of certain light music composers under this heading, and yet nearly always find Ketèlbey's music in between that of say Kalinnikov and Khachaturian on the classical music shelves. The same is also true of the music of Eric Coates. I have been told however, that this alignment is done purely for ease of categorising such music!

(4) Some believe that the bastion of recognition as a "serious" composer comes only if the composer in question is listed in *Grove* - full name *New Grove Dictionary of Music and Musicians* - seen by many as the "Bible" of the world of classical music. Though Albert W. Ketèlbey was not allowed within its 'sacred' covers for many years, even this famous institution no longer disregards him, and in recent years has seen fit to include his name amongst those other famous composers whose music his was the joy to praise and perform.

(5) *Your Hundred Best Tunes*, the long running BBC 2 Radio programme of listeners classical favourites has regularly included *In a Monastery Garden*, and in the 1997 poll this came 64th. Those who would demean this poll as being by those who lack knowledge of music, should take note of the comments of the programme's producer, Maura Clarke, when writing in *The Times* on 22nd September 1997 she said, "The listeners are very committed, very traditional and really know their stuff about classical music. They are extremely knowledgeable about music, and many were introduced to the programme via their families when they were young".

At the end of the day, is much of this labelling just a play on words, and is too much of life wasted on such trivialities? Could this be borne out in that as *The Watermill* by Ronald Binge (1910 - 79) came 35th in the above poll, the pundits should now argue as to whether this is "classical" music? .....but hang on a minute!...... isn't he the one who started off as a musician in a silent movie cinema, before playing accordion in Mantovani's orchestra; creating the "cascading strings" effect in that orchestra; and writing *Elizabethan Seranade* and *Sailing By*, which millions have grown to love ...... lets just call him the "Present King of Light Music". If we let it, that's how silly this whole facade can become, and perhaps the wiser words of Peter Gammond are helpful in bringing this whole matter back into focus, when writing on Ketèlbey's music in 1977 he simply said, "The music of Ketèlbey has lasted because it was well written and constructed, the fruit of a thorough musical education and wide experience in the commercial world of music".

EPILOGUE

FROM THE SANCTUARY OF HIS HEART

Forgetting ills behind me, the sorrows past and gone,
Forgetting all my wonderings, too sad to dwell upon,
Remembering God's great goodness, in times of stress and strain,
Remembering His restorings, I praise my God again.

Forgetting all unkindness which friends and foes have shown,
Forgetting and forgiving the wrongs that I have known,
Remembering God provided, unsought each faithful friend,
Remembering loves devotion, I'll praise Him to the end.

A. G.

*T*he saying goes, **"It is nice to be important, but it is far more important to be nice!"** Like all of us Albert W. Ketèlbey was human and far from perfect, but he never forgot the meagreness of his own beginnings, so that when he was rich and famous he very much "lived" the truth of the above words.

From what we have observed of his life we know that although he became rich at a comparatively young age, his real heart was not inclined to the glamour and grand life style he could have chosen to take from the world. Although he appreciated and enjoyed the advances in comfort and the opportunities to travel abroad which his wealth afforded him, his consistent ambition was to lead a quiet life in a peaceful and lovely home with a wife he adored, where he could work at the business of what he enjoyed doing most - composing his music, and in all that he ever did this is what he treasured most. (1 Thess. Ch. 4 v 11).

His generosity in financially helping others whenever he could came, I believe, from a compassionate heart, of one who saw "other things" of far more significance than material wealth, perhaps having some bearing on the fact that when he died, although he provided well for his widow, he did not leave what would be regarded as a fortune by today's standards. In October 1974 William Neve visited the composer's widow Mabel at her home at 202

Baring Road, West Cowes, and found her very reluctant to talk about her late husband. She said that she had promised 'Ket' that in his life time nothing should be allowed to bother him, and that he had no desire for anything to be written about him. According to Mabel, "he had a well stocked mind right to the end of his life", and that just before he died he had been studying again the Russian language, which he had first begun to study some twenty years earlier in 1939 - such was his resolve. Mabel was to survive him by more than twenty years, dying suddenly from a cerebral haemorrhage, whilst at home in Cowes on 15th October 1980, aged 76. Her late husband's generous heart had perhaps had its warm influence upon her own, for a kind instruction in her will meant that future royalties from sales of works and future earnings from performing rights, were to be divided equally between the Musicians Benevolent Fund and the Performing Right Society Members (Charitable) Fund.

He loved giving gifts at every opportune moment of his life to express his appreciation of friendships made, as vouched for by such as Harry Burgess and Paddy Dunn, who cherished personally inscribed cigarette boxes he presented to them. As a man of few words, those that are on record are in the main, with the exception of when he felt riled by his critics, either words of goodness about others rather than himself, or words of wit and humour tending to demean himself and bring a smile to the face of others. (Luke Ch. 6 vs. 37-38).

I have often been asked the question "Was Ketèlbey a religious man?" or "Do you think Ketèlbey was a Christian?" to which I have honestly answered "I don't know"; albeit in the times into which he was born, Christian morality stood for much more that it does today, and for many, church going was just a natural part of life. In once speaking of the time when he wrote *In a Monastery Garden*, he said something very interesting when referring to the necessity to feel what he wrote and have the right kind of inspiration, saying "in my early days I had had ascetic inclinations so it was not difficult to get myself into a suitable frame of mind". When William Neve raised the question of religion with Doris Ketelbey, she said of her brother, "No I don't thing he was religious in any ordinary or confirming sense, except that his mind and spirit were concentrated on transcendental and imaginative matters - but all artists have that kind of religion. He had this vivid creative imagination. He had it seems to me, a pictorial mind - he should have been a painter - and a consummate technical power of translating religious evocations into musical terms and cadences - but it didn't matter whether it was monks and Gregorian chants, or Chinese or Indians". We do know of course that earlier in his life he was involved in the church, firstly as a choir boy and then as a teenager, as church organist. There is no doubt, therefore, that some Christian influence came to bear on his life and likewise into much of his music, which, even at its light hearted extreme, in comparison to discordant, disordered and confused 'modern' classical music (if only to us ordinary mortals), always spelled an air of order, love and peace (1 Corinthians Ch. 14 v 33a), traits intensified in their evidence in his more serious music. How apposite here that when the German conductor and critic A. von Gizycki (Arkadjew) wrote of Ketèlbey's music in January 1930, he said, "Whenever I look through Ketèlbey's works, I always have the feeling that he has not quite achieved great symphonies, he has not had the gift of weight, of radiant power, of the really long line, so he has resigned himself to devoting his ability to a sort of orchestral art-in-miniature. Ketèlbey's directness, even a certain simplicity, are here the servants of a highly skilled composer. His music does not excite, but rather stimulates the spirit. It does not overwhelm us, but calms us".

If the above questions could be answered or these virtues embraced in all of their fullness in the Ketèlbey style, then surely such was done when at his pinnacle in 1924 he produced, what I believe is his masterpiece, what he called his *Mediation Religieuse - Sanctuary of the Heart*. No amusing pictures painted here, but simply what was at the heart of the man himself! As one previous writer once said "No mistaking that the heart is worn firmly on the sleeve here", and another "It aims straight at the common man's solar plexus - and scores a bulls eye!"

As the Psalms of David and the silent but real presence of friends and loved ones have brought solace and comfort to those who are heart broken, so too I believe this beautiful musical meditation has done so over the years. From beginning to end it calmly expresses a human heart's desire and longing for tenderness, love and compassion, and such expressions and sentiments of the heart of the composer were surely exemplified when he added these words to be sung by soloist and full choir:-

I wander'd alone in a strange land,
And Life was so dark and drear,
When the sound of a voice seemed to call me
And brought to my mind a mem'ry dear;
It told of the Joy and the Gladness
That comes from the One above, -
"Oh Lord, hear our prayer,
Take away all our care,
And fill all our hearts with Love."

The sound of solemn chanting
Was borne to me from afar,
And the song seemed to draw me closer,
Like the light of a guiding star;
I turned from out the highway
To the Minster old and grey,
And the voices swelled in welcome
For a stranger come to pray.

My Soul was enthralled by the Message
That came from those voices clear,
And my Heart found a shelter and comfort
From the pain of this world so dark and drear;
I *knew* then, the Joy and the Gladness
As I prayed to the One above,
"Oh Lord, hear our prayer
Take away all our care,
And fill all our hearts with love.

> Oh Lord have mercy upon us,
> And upon all those who pray
> To Thee, our Father
> Who heareth us this day
> Oh Lord have mercy upon us,
> And upon all those who pray
> Oh Lord, hear our prayer
> Take away all our care,
> And fill all our hearts with love".
> Amen, Amen.

There are possibly references within this song to certain Psalms of the Bible. From his earlier association with the Church of England, Ketèlbey would have been familiar with the Book of Common Prayer and in this context with one chant called *Tonus Peregrinus*. This means "wanderer tune" and is based on Psalm 114, the two opening verses of which are, "When Israel went out of Egypt, the house of Jacob from a people of strange language; Judah was his sanctuary, and Israel his dominion". Likewise in the well known *By the rivers of Babylon* Psalm 137, the fourth verse reads, "How shall we sing the LORD'S song in a strange land?" But why does Ketèlbey use as the basis of the second theme within this work an ancient Hebrew melody known as the Kol Nidrei? [23] Bearing in mind Lottie and her family's Jewish roots and his own Christian upbringing, was the inclusion of the Kol Nidrei part of his own desire to unite biblical references to exile, escape and even diaspora with both Jewish and Christian teaching on redemption? [24]

As interesting and true as all of this may be, I believe his words to *Sanctuary of the Heart* have far deeper and personal meaning. The Psalms and chants referred to above are set in the plural, but "the heart" of this song is set very much in the singular, and these surely are not just words inspired by liturgy and theology. Neither are they words of casual acquaintance or doubt, but rather, I believe, of a hymn and prayer of one who had tasted the goodness and grace of God. And even here are there undertones of that broken relationship with his father, so exposing his most poignant feelings - the heartbreak of "losing" his earthly father and the joy and reconciliation of a burdened heart finding his heavenly one? (Psalm 16 vs. 9 - 11).

In this respect I find it interesting and quite touching to note, that in writing these words, and in particular the fifth line of the last verse, the composer purposely set the word 'knew' in italics to distinguish it from all other words in the complete song! I for one am so glad that he "slaughtered some of those innocents", for surely in so doing his was the gift to give them a lighter yet fuller life, with all the musical colour he could muster up, to give us those unaffected melodies of the monastery garden, God's sunny open countryside, the moonlight and the Orient, yes and even the sanctuary of the heart of the man himself.

---

23 Meaning *Break All Vows*, an Hebraic prayer chant used in the Jewish liturgy on the Eve of the Day of Atonement.

24 Information drawn from Tom McCanna's notes written for music album *Ketèlbey Classics for Piano*. Pub. Bosworth & Co. Ltd. 1999.

Chronology including Ketèlbey's compositions
referred to in this book (shown in italics).

1875   9th August: Born 41 Alma Street, Aston Manor.

1880   Musical talent realised. (circa 1880)

1883   Begins piano lessons with W. Newey. (circa 1883)

1884   Becomes choirboy at St. Silas' Church, Lozells. (circa 1884)

1886   Becomes student at the recently established School of
Music of the Birmingham and Midland Institute.

1888   Is the only student to gain a first class pass in examinations
in Advanced Harmony. *Sonata for Pianoforte*

1889   Wins Queen Victoria Scholarship for Composition at Trinity
College of Music, London.
27th June: Articles of Pupilship signed with Trinity College of
Music. Goes to London where he continues his formal education at
Fitzroy College, where he is also a boarder.
16th August: Performs at private concert, Barford Road Board
Schools, Birmingham.
Goes into approved lodgings at the home of Mr. & Mrs. Alfred
Hoare.

1890   Wins Turner Pianoforte Medal at Trinity College.

1892   *Caprice for Piano and Orchestra* Wins again Queen Victoria
Scholarship for Composition and appointed organist at St. John's
Church, Wimbledon.
Overture Wins College Medals for Harmony and Counterpoint and
the Gabriel Prize.

1893   *Concertstück for Piano and Orchestra* (circa 1893)

1894   Appointed Associate of Trinity College of Music.
Rêverie; Romance for piano and violin (or cello)

1895   *Piano Concerto in G Minor* Wins Tallis Gold Medal for
Counterpoint**.** Appointed Licentiate of Trinity College of Music.

1896 *String Quartet* (circa 1896); *Quintet for Oboe, Clarinet, Bassoon, Horn and Piano* (circa 1896) for which he wins the Sir Michael Costa Prize and the College Gold Medal. *Orchestral Suite in Three Movements; Every Good Gift* (anthem); *Behold Upon the Mountains* (anthem); *Be Strong! All ye People* (anthem) Takes up post as conductor of travelling light opera company.

1898 23rd June: Gives recital of several of his works at Trinity College of Music. Appointed Musical Director of Opera Comique and moves into 13 Bruton Street. *Blow! blow! thou winter wind* (song)

1899 December 1898 to March 1899 "Alice in Wonderland" at Opera Comique. April to May "A Good Time" at Opera Comique. *There's something in the English after all!* (song); *Under the Starlight* (song); *In Sweet Disguise* (song); *The Knight's Return* (song); *The Heavenly Message* (song)
Meets Miss Charlotte Siegenberg.

1900 *The Wonder Worker* - comic opera in the style of Gilbert and Sullivan which is staged at the Grand Theatre, Fulham.
Begins transcription work for the music publishing company Hammond & Co. (circa 1900)

1902 *Kildoran* (song)

1903 *Six Musical Impressions for Piano; Scherzo de Concert for Flute and Piano*

1904 Begins transcription work for the music publishing company Chappell & Co.

1905 *Six Original Pieces without Octaves* (circa 1905)

1906 27th August: Marries Charlotte Siegenberg at St. Giles' Register Office, London, and the couple go to live at 42 (Upper) Bedford Place, Bloomsbury.

1907 Joins Columbia Graphophone Company Ltd. as their Impresario. *Alice in Wonderland - Four characteristic pieces for Piano Op. 20; The Heart's Awakening* (song); *At Parting* (song)

1909 Makes his first recording as artist with Columbia as solo organist in Handel's 'Hallelujah' from "Messiah". *My Heart A-dream* (song) Moves home to 73 Cromwell Road, Kensington.

1910 Begins transcription work for the music publishing company Elkin & Co. *Prelude in C Sharp Minor*

1912 15th February: Inaugural performance of *The Phantom Melody* for which he wins Auguste Van Biene Cello Competition and £50.00 prize sponsored by Tit-Bits Magazine.
I Loved you more than I knew (song)

1913 April: Inaugural performance of *Suite de Ballet*.
23rd November: Inaugural performance of *My Heart still clings to You* (song) for which he wins the first prize of £100.00 in the Evening News Song Competition. *Berceuse*

1914 The couple move to live at 57 Springfield Road, St. John's Wood. *Keep your Toys, Laddie Boy!* (song); *Rapsodie sérieuse; The trumpet -voice of Motherland is calling* (song); *The Old Ingle-nook* (song)

1915 *In a Monastery Garden; A Dream Picture; Silver Cloud; Tangled Tunes; Fiddle Fun; "Kinema Music" e.g. Quiet River Scene - Love - Romance; Pathetic - Relating to Sad Story etc; Mexican or Spanish*, being music for the silent movies. *Mind the Slide!*

1916 *"New Moving Picture Book" e.g. Plaintive, Oriental Music, Hurry Music, Mysterioso* being music for the silent movies.
Begins working for Andre Charlot at the Vaudeville Theatre as Musical Director for the Revue "Samples!". *Pastorale*

1917 *Fairy Butterfly* (song)

1918 Becomes member of the Performing Right Society.

1919 Bosworth & Co. become his main publisher.
In the Moonlight

1920 *Wedgwood Blue; In a Persian Market*

1921   Moves home to 15 Frognal, Hampstead.
Bells across the Meadows; Evening Calm; Gallantry; A Desert Romance; Reflections; Sunset Glow

1922   *Romantic Suite; The Shadow of Dreams*

1923   July: Involved in the legal proceedings over copyright known as the "Polly Case".
In a Chinese Temple Garden; A Musical Jig-saw; Christmas; Golden Autumn

1924   10th April: First performance of *Suite romantique. Chal Romano Overture; Will you forgive* (song); *Sanctuary of the Heart; Love's Devotion; Cockney Suite; Schmetterling; "Bosworth's Loose Leaf Film - Play Series" (Books 1 and 2) e.g. True Love, Arabian Nights, Agitato furioso, Mysterious*

1925   Moves home to 15 Lindfield Gardens, Hampstead.
"Bosworth's Loose-leaf Film - Play Series" (Book 3); In a Lovers' Garden; In a Camp of the Ancient Britons; Algerian Scene

1926   Sheet music sales of *In a Monastery Garden* top 1,000,000. (circa 1926) Following dispute with the Performing Right Society he resigns his membership, but rejoins later. The critics begin their onslaught in ridiculing his music. *Jungle Drums; A Dream of Christmas; Butterfly's Frolic* Resigns from his post with Columbia Graphophone Co. Ltd. by which time he had risen to become their Musical Director and Adviser. The organist Reginald Foort makes popular recording of *In a Monastery Garden* and *In a Persian Market.*

1927   April: Inaugural performance of *Three Fanciful Etchings.*
23rd September: Inaugural performance of *In a Fairy Realm.*
By the Blue Hawaiian Waters

1928   Begins authentic composer recordings with Columbia of 16 of his most popular works, viz "Ketelbey conducting his Concert Orchestra".

1929   *The Sacred Hour* Extensive European concert tour.
"The Jazz Singer" brings to an end the era of silent movies.

1930 8th February: Inaugural performance of *The Clock and the Dresden Figures* at the Kingsway Hall, London, in what is to be the first of annual Ketèlbey concerts held here.
The use of radio and gramophone as a relaxing medium by the masses intensifies.
His association with the Royal Military School of Music, Kneller Hall begins.

1931 11th April: Inaugural performance of *The Vision of Fuji-San* and *Knights of the King* (march).
Summer: Packed schedule of concerts in his U.K. tour. *In the Mystic Land of Egypt; Sunday Afternoon Reverie*

1932 *Dance of the Merry Mascots; A Birthday Greeting* The success and popularity of his summer concert tours reach their peak.
September: Extensive concert tour in Holland.
Peter Dawson records song version of *In a Monastery Garden*.

1934 *My Lady Brocade* 8th May: King George V acclaims *A State Procession* - the first movement of *Cockney Suite*.

1935 9th February: First public performance of *With Honour Crowned* (march). *With the Roumanian Gypsies* Marches incorporated within Pageants at the Aldershot Military Tattoo (continuing each year through to 1938).

1937 *Royal Cavalcade* (march); *A Mayfair Cinderella* (song); *I Dream of all the Worlds* (song)

1938 12th February: Inaugural performance of *Sunbeams and Butterflies* and *In Holiday Mood*.

1939 May: Musical Opinion journal reports "A Ketèlbey night means "house full" for the "King of Light Music" is exceedingly popular with orchestras and audiences alike".

1941 *Fighting for Freedom* (marching song)

1945 18th November: Inaugural performance of *The Adventurers*.

1946 *King Cupid* (song)

1947   20th February: Charlotte dies from pneumonia at Regents Park Nursing Home.   Sells home and moves into Hendon Hall Hotel. Suffers nervous breakdown and so convalesces in hotels on south coast.   Summer "come-back" concert at Worthing.   Meets Mrs. Mabel Maud Pritchett. *Caprice Pianistique; Skitty Kitty; Birthday of the Little Princess*

1948   30th October: Marries Mabel Maud Pritchett at Bournemouth Register Office, and goes to live at Harbour Mount, Bembridge, I.O.W.

1949   Moves home to "Rookstone", Egypt Hill, West Cowes. BBC snub his music in their 'Festival of Light Music'. *Angelo d'amore; My Star of Love* (song)

1950   21st July: First performance of *Italian Twilight.*

1951   *On Brading Down*

1952   5th June: *With Honour Crowned* played as slow march at Trooping the Colour ceremony, whilst the Queen inspected the parade.

1953   11th June: *With Honour Crowned* played as slow march at Trooping the Colour ceremony, whilst the Queen inspected the parade.
5th August: Appears on Eric Robinson's popular television programme 'Music for You'.

1957   Interviewed by Barry Westwood on Southern Television.

1959   Moves home to 41 Osborne Court, Parade, West Cowes. *The Swiss Dancing Doll*
26th November: Dies at 41 Osborne Court.
1st December: Cremated at Golders Green Crematorium, North London.

A DISCOGRAPHY OF KETÈLBEY'S
MUSIC ON COMPACT DISCS
(NOT EXHAUSTIVE)

**Including the author's own thoughts and
comments on each disc listed.**

Title: *"The Grand Passions of ALBERT W. KETÈLBEY"*.

CHANDOS Flyback Label. 1998   FBCD 2002 DDD

Artists: The Palm Court Theatre Orchestra conducted by Anthony Godwin.

(1)   *In the Moonlight*

(2)   *In a Persian Market*

(3)   *Bells across the Meadows*

       Cockney Suite:-

       (4)   *A State Procession (Buckingham Palace)*
       (5)   *The Cockney Lover (Lambeth Walk)*
       (6)   *At the Palais de Danse (Anywhere)*
       (7)   *Elegy (Thoughts on passing the Cenotaph)*
       (8)   *Bank Holiday ('Appy 'Ampstead)*

(9)   *Wedgwood Blue*

(10)   *The Clock and the Dresden Figures*

       Suite: In a Lovers' Garden:-

       (11)   *A Song of Love*
       (12)   *The Golden Wedding*
       (13)   *A Garden Fête*

(14)   *In a Chinese Temple Garden*

(15)   *Sanctuary of the Heart*

(16)   *Jungle Drums*

An excellent recording of some of Ketèlbey's popular works played in typical Palm Court style, which was so popular in the 1920s and 1930s. Of particular note is a charming performance of his *Suite: In a Lovers' Garden* and a rare performance of *Jungle Drums*.

Title: *"the world of Ketèlbey"*

DECCA Label. 1997   452 987-2 ADD (tracks 10 to 14 MONO)

Re-issue of 1959 recordings tracks 1 to 9, and 1954 recordings tracks 10 to 14.

Artists: The New Symphony Orchestra of London conducted by Robert Sharples (tracks 1 to 9).
   The New Symphony Orchestra conducted by Stanford Robinson (tracks 10 to 14).

(1)   *In a Monastery Garden*

(2)   *Wedgwood Blue*

(3)   *In a Chinese Temple Garden*

(4)   *Sanctuary of the Heart*

(5)   *'Appy 'Ampstead*

(6)   *In a Persian Market*

(7)   *The Phantom Melody*

(8)   *Bells across the Meadows*

(9)   *In the Mystic Land of Egypt*

(10) *The Ploughman Homeward Plods his Weary Way*

(11) *A Passing Storm on a Summer Day*

(12) *By the Blue Hawaiian Waters*

(13) *In the Moonlight*

(14) *With Honour Crowned*

   Tracks 1 to 9 form the CD issue of the first LP recording of Ketèlbey's music I ever bought in the early 1970s and introduced me to the composer, and therefore all have special meaning to me, *Bells across the Meadows* being the finest performance I have ever heard. Although tracks 10 to 14 are Mono, they are brilliantly performed under the baton of Stanford Robinson, and particularly so with Ketèlbey's inspiring march *With Honour Crowned*.

Title: ***"In a Monastery Garden.***
          The Immortal Works of Albert Ketèlbey"

DECCA LONDON Label. 1996   444 786-2 ADD

Re-issue of 1969 recordings tracks 1 to 9.
Artists: Royal Philharmonic Orchestra & Chorus conducted by Eric Rogers.

Tracks 10 - 18 (re-issue of 1972 recordings)
VARIOUS VIOLIN ENCORES.
Artists: London Festival Orchestra, Josef Sakonov violin.

(1)   *In a Monastery Garden*

(2)   *Wedgwood Blue*

(3)   *In the Mystic Land of Egypt*

(4)   *Bells across the Meadows*

(5)   *In a Chinese Temple Garden*

(6)   *Sanctuary of the Heart*

(7)   *'Appy 'Ampstead*

(8)   *The Phantom Melody*

(9)   *In a Persian Market*

Tracks 1 to 9 became a very popular LP recording when it was issued in 1969, and the Royal Philharmonic Orchestra and Chorus give a fine performance of the works under Eric Rogers. Particularly good are their renderings of *In the Mystic Land of Egypt* and *'Appy 'Ampstead* - though in this the use of a modern organ in place of mouth organs does not sound quite right!

Included in the Violin Encores (track 15) is a beautiful arrangement for solo violin and orchestra of Richard Heuberger's famous *Opera Ball Waltz*.

Title: **"CLASSICS FOR PLEASURE - MUSIC OF KETÈLBEY"**

EMI Label. 1993   CFP 4637 ADD

Re-issue of 1977 recordings tracks 1 to 9.

Artists: Philharmonia Orchestra, Ambrosian Singers, Vernon Midgley - Tenor, Jean Temperley - Mezzo-Soprano, Leslie Pearson - Piano, conducted by John Lanchbery.

Tracks 10 - 13 (re-issue of 1959 recordings) Selections from *BALLET SUITE: EGYPTIEN, OP 12*. LUIGINI.

Artists: Royal Philharmonic Orchestra Conducted by Anatole Fistoulari.

(1)   *In a Persian Market*

(2)   *In a Monastery Garden*

(3)   *Chal Romano (Gipsy Lad)*

(4)   *In the Mystic Land of Egypt*

(5)   *The Clock and the Dresden Figures*

(6)   *Bells across the Meadows*

(7)   *In a Chinese Temple Garden*

(8)   *In the Moonlight*

(9)   *Sanctuary of the Heart*

This performance and interpretation of some of Ketèlbey's popular works under the direction of the Australian composer/conductor John Lanchbery, is, with the exception of *Bells across the Meadows*, the best I have ever heard, and the rendering of *Sanctuary of the Heart* with the Ambrosian Singers and the brilliant mezzo-soprano Jean Temperley, would I believe even make the hair on the back of Ketèlbey's neck stand up!

Title: **"British Light Music - Albert KETÈLBEY"**

Marco Polo Label. 1992   8.223442 DDD

Artists: Czecho-Slovak Radio Symphony Orchestra (Bratislava). Slovak Philharmonic Male Chorus conducted by Adrian Leaper.

(1) *In a Monastery Garden*

(2) *Overture: The Adventurers*

(3) *Chal Romano (Gipsy Lad)*

 Suite romantique:-

  (4) *Romance*
  (5) *Scherzo*
  (6) *Valse dramatique*

(7) *Caprice Pianistique*

(8) *The Clock and the Dresden Figures*

(9) *'Appy 'Ampstead*

(10) *At the Palais de Danse*

(11) *In the Moonlight*

(12) *Wedgwood Blue*

(13) *Bells across the Meadows*

(14) *The Phantom Melody*

(15) *In a Persian Market*

 A good all round performance of some of Ketèlbey's popular works, together with the more serious *Suite romantique* and the little known *Overture: The Adventurers*. The flamboyant *Caprice Pianistique* is given a particularly good performance, as is the beautiful *Phantom Melody*, and the Slovak Philharmonic Male Chorus make an excellent contribution to the first and last tracks.

Title: *"Ketèlbey"*

PHILIPS Virtuoso Label. 1999   400 011-2 DDD

Re-issue of 1982 recordings previously issued on CD (with same number) by PHILIPS, but under their Digital Classics Label.

Artists: London Promenade Orchestra, Ambrosian Chorus, Laurence Dale - Tenor, Michael Reeves - Piano, conducted by Alexander Faris.

(1)   *In a Chinese Temple Garden*

(2)   *In a Monastery Garden*

(3)   *Sanctuary of the Heart*

(4)   *'Appy 'Ampstead*

(5)   *Dance of the Merry Mascots*

(6)   *In a Persian Market*

(7)   *In the Mystic Land of Egypt*

(8)   *Bells across the Meadows*

(9)   *The Clock and the Dresden Figures*

(10)   *With Honour Crowned*

Another good all round performance of some of Ketèlbey's popular works, including a now rare performance of his jolly *Dance of the Merry Mascots*.

Title: ***"ALBERT W. KETÈLBEY"***

Pearl Label. 1992   GEMM CD 9968 AAD (MONO)

(1)   *In a Persian Market*

(2)   *Wedgwood Blue*

(3)   *Chal Romano (Gipsy Lad)*

(4)   *In a Monastery Garden*

(5)   *The Clock and the Dresden Figures*

(6)   *Bells across the Meadows*

        Suite: In Holiday Mood:-

        (7)   *On the Promenade*
        (8)   *Down the Stream*
        (9)   *The Illuminated Fête*

(10)   *A Musical Jig-Saw*

(11)   *A Birthday Greeting*

(12)   *Algerian Scene*

(13)   *'Appy 'Ampstead*

(14)   *Sunbeams and Butterflies*

(15)   *Knights of the King*

(16)   *At the Palais de Danse*

(17)   *In a Camp of the Ancient Britons*

An excellent re-recording of vintage 78s supplied from the collection of the late Stuart Upton of the Vintage Light Music Society (now sadly disbanded). Artists include Peter Dawson, Clifford Greenwood, Albert Sandler and Monia Liter, with the composer himself conducting his own Concert Orchestra on tracks 1, 3, 6, 13, 16 & 17 and playing the piano parts on tracks 2 and 5, with the same orchestra, and track 12 with Albert Sandler. This is the CD to go for if you are after genuine composer performance recordings.

Title: **KETÈLBEY Piano Music Vol.1**

Marco Polo Label. 1995   8.223699 DDD

Artist: Rosemary Tuck.

(1) *In the Woodlands*	(13) *The voice of the trees*
(2) *Impromptu No. 1*	(14) *Poor little bird*
(3) *Pensée fantastique*	(15) *Oh! Look at the rabbits!*
(4) *Reflections*	(16) *Listen! What's that?*
(5) *Mirror Dance*	(17) *I do love you*
(6) *A Song of Summer*	(18) *Let's play at Indians!*
(7) *Golden Autumn*	(19) *Let's hurry home,*
(8) *Daffodils*	*it's getting dark*
(9) *Sunset Glow*	(20) *Angelo d'amore*
(10) *Valse caprice*	(21) *A River Rêverie*
(11) *The Shadow of Dreams*	(22) *La grâcieuse*
(12) *This is where the*	(23) *In a Monastery Garden*
fairies dance	

Title: **KETÈLBEY Piano Music Vol.2**

Marco Polo Label. 1995   8.223700 DDD

Artist: Rosemary Tuck.

(1) *Rapsodie sérieuse*	(12) *Swing Song*
(2) *Pastorale*	(13) *Galop brilliante*
(3) *A Romantic Melody*	(14) *Rêverie*
(4) *La joie de vivre*	(15) *The Pilgrims*
(5) *Légende triste*	(16) *On the Volga*
(6) *Pensées joyeuses*	(17) *Le chant des orphelins*
(7) *Rêverie dramatique*	(18) *A Dream Picture*
(8) *The Mill*	(19) *Valse lyrique*
(9) *Polonaise*	(20) *Morceau pathétique*
(10) *Berceuse*	(21) *Prelude in C Sharp Minor*
(11) *Chanson del la tristesse*	(22) *Valse brillante*

Every Ketèlbey fan should own these. Rosemary's brilliant performance and beautiful interpretation of these works, are epitomised in words she once wrote to me in a letter expressing her opinions of the composer's music, when she said, "To me, it is Ketèlbey's heartfelt use of melody, tinged with harmonies that contribute to its essence, that give the music its genuine sincerity".

TEN OF KETÈLBEY'S CONTEMPORARIES OF BRITISH LIGHT MUSIC AND SOME OF THEIR POPULAR COMPOSITIONS

RICHARD ADDINSELL 1904 - 1977

Warsaw Concerto, Smokey Mountain Concerto, The Prince and the Showgirl, Blithe Spirit, Greengage Summer.

RONALD BINGE 1910 - 1979

Elizabethan Serenade, The Watermill, Sailing By, Concerto for Alto Saxophone, The Whispering Valley, Trade Winds.

ERIC COATES 1886 - 1957

London Suite, Calling All Workers, By the Sleepy Lagoon, The Dam Busters March, Saxo-Rhapsody, The Three Bears, The Three Elizabeths, Last Love, Under the Stars.

SAMUEL COLERIDGE-TAYLOR 1875 - 1912

Hiawatha, Gipsy Suite, Petite Suite, Othello Suite, The Bamboula.

FREDERIC CURZON 1899 - 1973

The Boulevardier, Robin Hood Suite, Dance of an Ostracised Imp, Punchinello, Bravada - Pasa Doble, Cascade Waltz.

EDWARD GERMAN 1862 - 1936

Merrie England, Tom Jones, Gipsy Suite, Nell Gwyn, Romeo and Juliet, The Conqueror.

ARCHIBALD JOYCE 1873 - 1963

Dreaming, A Thousand Kisses, Dreams of You, Acushla, Passing of Salome, The Brighton Hike, Prince of Wales March.

ROGER QUILTER 1877 - 1953

A Children's Overture, Where the Rainbow Ends, As You Like It, The Rake, Three English Dances.

SYDNEY TORCH 1908 - 1990

Petite Valse, Trapeze Waltz, Samba Sud, Shortcake - Walk, London Transport Suite, Bicycle Belles, Cresta Run.

HAYDN WOOD 1882 - 1959

Mayday Overture, Roses of Picardy, Sketch of a Dandy, A Manx Rhapsody, An Evening Song, The Horse Guards, Joyousness Waltz.

BIBLIOGRAPHY

Books & Directories:-

Birmingham City Council. *Developing Birmingham 1889 to 1989.*
  pub. Development Department, Birmingham City Council 1989.

Dinn, Freda. *The Observers Book of Music.*
  pub. Frederick Warne & Co. 1966.

Ehrlich, Cyril. *Harmonious Alliance - A History of the Performing Right Society.*
  pub. Oxford University Press 1989.

Gammond, Peter. *The Oxford Companion to Popular Music.*
  pub. Oxford University Press 1991.

Ganzl, Kurt. *The British Musical Theatre.*
  pub. Macmillan 1986.

Godfrey, Sir Dan. *Memories and Music.*
  pub. Hutchinson & Co. 1924.

Handford, Margaret. *Sounds Unlikely - Six Hundred Years of Music in Birmingham.*
  pub. The Birmingham and Midland Institute 1992.

Hogarth, Basil. *Albert W. Ketèlbey - A Master of Melody.*
  pub. Bosworth & Co.

Inglis, Simon. *Villa Park - One Hundred Years.*
  pub. Sports Projects 1997.

Martland, Peter. *Since Records Began - EMI The First 100 Years.*
  pub. B.T. Batsford 1997.

McCanna, Tom. *The Music of Albert W. Ketèlbey.*
  pub. Tom McCanna 1998.

Price, Victor. *Aston Remembered.*
  pub. Brewin Books 1991.

Robinson, Eric. *Conducted Personally.*
   pub. Stanley Paul & Co. 1955.

Scowcroft, Philip. *British Light Music.*
   pub. Thames 1997.

Taylor, Ronald. *Columbia Twelve-Inch Records in the United Kingdom -
   A Discography.*
   pub. Symposium Records 1994.

Turner, Major Gordon. *The History of British Military Bands.*
   pub. Spellmount 1997.

Young, Kenneth. *Music's Great Days in the Spas and Watering Places.*
   pub. Macmillan 1968.

New Grove Dictionary of Music & Musicians.
   pub. Macmillan 1980.

Who's Who in Music.
   pub Pitman 1915.

Who's Who.
   pub. A & C Black 1995.

Kelly's Directories.
   pub. Kelly's Directories (Various years).

Hulley's Directories.
   pub. J. Hulley (Various years).

Newspapers, Magazines, Journals, etc:-

Birmingham Evening Mail.
Birmingham Post. 27th November 1959.
Birmingham Evening Despatch. 1st September 1928 & 9th May 1934.
The Birmingham Weekly Post. 7th June 1935.
Birmingham Gazette. 11th May 1934.
Birmingham Voice.

Daily Telegraph. 26th July 1954.

Daily Express. 6th August 1953.

The Times. 27th November 1959.

The Sunday Times. 2nd August 1959.

The Weston Mercury. 9th August 1924.

Surrey Comet. 24th December 1935.

The Brighton Herald.

The Brighton Gazette.

Brighton and Hove Herald.

The Southend Standard.

Sunday Daily News.

Blackpool Evening Gazette. 2nd September 1948.

Isle of Wight County Press. 28th November 1959.

Radio Times. 4th September 1931.

The Musical Mirror. June 1921.

The Musical Times. 1st June 1898 & 1st November 1927.

The British Musician. February 1896 & December 1896.

Musical Opinion.

Musical Opinion and Music Trade Review.

Music Masterpieces. 18th March 1926.

The Talking Machine and Wireless Trade News. July 1928.

Vintage Light Music.

The Sound Wave. October 1932.

Der Artist (Dusseldorf). 31st January 1930.

The Gramophone.

The Lady. 21st August 1975.

Cotswold Life. January 1976.

The Islander (I.O.W.). April 1991.

Provincial Bulletin. (Of the Order of Franciscan Friars Minor).June 1967.

The Musical Progress and Mail. September 1935.

The Military Musician. October 1935.

A CONCISE BIOGRAPHY OF THE

VIRTUOSO VIOLINIST

HAROLD GEORGE KETÈLBEY

1883 - 1965

There are those who work in the spheres of art, science, medicine and religion, whose endeavours and achievements make this world a better and richer place, yet who in return in this life, are given little or no honour and glory.

More often than not being of meek character seems to be, or have been, their portion, but He who sweat blood and was the epitome of meekness has declared that those of such character will inherit the earth.

Henry Robbins.

With a young family to rear, as we have seen, it was not always financially easy for George and Sarah to launch their son Albert into his musical career, and therefore when their youngest son, also at a very young age began to show remarkable talent on George's favourite musical instrument - the violin, his parents were placed in somewhat of a dilemma. Such was the boy's talent and keenness, however, that in 1889 at just 6 years of age Harold George Ketèlbey made his first public appearance on the concert platform, whereby his parents then knew that they could not deny him the opportunity such talent deserved, and allowed him the lessons he needed to take. By the age of 12 he was performing regularly at matinee concerts of the Birmingham Royal Society of Artists, and it was whilst performing at these concerts that he was spotted by a certain Oscar Pollack, the musical critic of the *Birmingham Daily Mail*, who was very impressed by the boy's playing, and believed he had great promise. Such was his interest in seeing young Harold develop the natural talent he possessed, that it was Pollack who was instrumental in obtaining for him a scholarship at the School of Music of the Birmingham and Midland Institute, which brother Albert had earlier attended. Here he became a pupil of Max Mossel and studied alongside Marie Hall (1884 - 1956) the world famous violinist.

Harold went from strength to strength in his studies, and brought much pride to his family when on 3rd October 1900 as a 17 year old violinist he was one of the youngest members of the orchestra for the inaugural performance of Sir Edward Elgar's *The Dream of Gerontius* at Birmingham Town Hall during the Birmingham Triennial Musical Festival of that year, and for which Elgar had been commissioned to write the full scale oratorio. At the end of the performance all members of the orchestra were asked to sign Elgar's manuscript of the composition, which all, and indeed other dignitaries present at the performance, were delighted to do, and which Elgar presented to the Oratory in Birmingham on the 17th September 1902, in memory of Cardinal Newman on whose poem he had based the work. Included in the signatures on the manuscript are Harold, and also his teacher Max Mossel, who was also a member of the orchestra.

Such was his achievement at the Birmingham School of Music that at the age of 19 he was appointed teacher of the violin there. After holding his teaching post for a year - during which time he gave three recitals of the music of his favourite composer, Johann Sebastian Bach (1685 - 1750) and having performed the remarkable feat of playing from beginning to end the three sonatas and three partitas for solo violin by Bach, representing nearly two hours playing, completely from memory - he resigned, and together with Marie Hall went to the Conservatory in Prague to become a pupil of the renowned Czech violinist and teacher Otakar Ševčik (1852 - 1934). Later when performing at a concert in Frankfurt, Germany, providence paved the way for further opportunity for Harold, when sitting in the audience was a Mrs. Desoff the widow of a previous Director of the Vienna and Frankfurt Opera House. So delighted was she with his playing that within a few days she had sent him an enthusiastic letter of introduction to the famous Hungarian violinist, teacher and composer Dr. Joseph Joachim (1831 - 1907) who was an intimate friend of the great composer - Johannes Brahms (1833 - 1897) and who as a boy performer himself was regularly accompanied in public by another great composer - Felix Mendelssohn (1809 - 1847).

Thus Harold went before the great man of the violin for assessment, and performed the *Pathetique Violin Concerto* by Heinrich Wilhelm Ernst (1814 - 1865) and Bach's beautiful *Chaconne*[25] from the *Partita No. 2 in D Minor for Solo Violin*, and having duly impressed the master was enrolled as a pupil under him at the Hochschule, Berlin. It was Joachim who was to have much influence upon the technique of Harold's violin playing, and who was to teach him his own unique and rather unorthodox way of bowing, which was in turn to remain as a trait of Harold's own playing for the remainder of his career.

Whilst studying in Berlin, he was invited to play before another "Great of the violin", the Belgian violinist, conductor and composer Eugène Ysaÿe (1858 -1931) who in response to his playing gave him an autographed photograph inscribed "A young artist of great talent and great future", and after completing his studies under Dr. Joachim, he was received with much acclaim when he gave a recital at the Bechstein Saal, Berlin in March 1905 at barely 22 years of age.

Whilst living in Berlin he met and married a German lady - Gertrude Anna Maria Tempelhagen who was then Professor of Physics at Berlin University, and the daughter of Hugo Tempelhagen, a Director of the famous German company Siemens - Aver. From Berlin his career brought the couple back to England to work in London, Eastbourne and Brighton. After a performance of Joachim's *Violin Concerto in Hungarian Style* at a concert in London in October 1909, the music critic of *The Times* said of his performance, "Mr. Ketèlbey has very strong artistic perception, backed by a well developed technique. He played with a fine and smooth tone and strong characteristic phrasing the whole of Joachim's *Hungarian Concerto*, and came through the trying ordeal exceedingly well. Few violinists have

---

25 It has been said that the *Chaconne* represents a virtual summation of the solo violin's expressive capabilities.

sufficient vitality to get through the long first movement without ever letting their interest flag........He rendered the difficult cadenza with remarkable accuracy and neatness which showed how high is his technical accomplishment."

It was, however, in Brighton where he and wife Gertrude settled down, and where their first child Catherine Friederik Johanna was born in 1913. By this time Harold had tried his own hand at composition, writing his own *Violin Concerto* and several songs, but it was his composition of several cadenzas to famous concertos which won him most admiration. He was now availing himself as a violin teacher once more for private lessons, one of his students being a Mr. Dench of Brighton who studied under his expertise for several months over the years 1912/13. His daughter Emily recalled in later years the excellence her father attached to Harold's teaching ability, and whose autographed photograph which Harold had given to his student, she still kept (see plate 6). In 1914 Henry Lyell-Tayler was appointed conductor of the Brighton Municipal Orchestra, and in knowing of Harold's ability and the fact that he was "on the doorstep", soon appointed him as leader of the orchestra. Lyell-Tayler was a highly respected musician of the time, a Midlander himself and a brilliant violinist, he had been the leader of Henry Wood's famous Promenade Orchestra and sometimes acting as Wood's deputy conductor.

After military service in the First World War, Harold returned home to continue his career as leader of the Brighton Municipal Orchestra - soon after to also be appointed by Lyell-Tayler as his deputy conductor, and within a few years circumstances at the other end of the world were to determine further developments in the career of Harold. During the early 1920s there had become an increasing desire amongst many people in Durban, South Africa to establish an orchestra there. Several dignitaries of the Durban Council were amongst those keen on this idea, and when (presumably through their influence) it was agreed that funding would be made available to establish and operate a Civic Orchestra there, the opportunity to set this up and running fell to none other than Henry Lyell-Tayler, who duly accepted the challenge, and persuaded Harold to join him as leader of the new orchestra. So it was that in 1923 with his wife Gertrude and daughter Catherine, he emigrated for a new life in South Africa, where in the same year the couple's second child Hugo Frank Werner (later known as Billy) was born.

By 1924 the orchestra of some forty musicians had been set up and was giving concerts, and not long after an old acquaintance of both Harold and H. Lyell-Tayler made contact with them. This was a certain Rev. Arnold

Pierce-Jones who when working in a parish in Brighton had been a regular season ticket holder for their Brighton concerts, but who himself had emigrated to Cape Town in 1921. In taking his first holiday break since arriving in Cape Town, he decided to go to Durban where he attended a civic concert given by the relatively new orchestra, and met again the two musicians for whom he had great admiration from those Brighton concert days. His memories of this Durban concert were of the continuing professionalism and brilliance of both men, the tall and broad figure of H. Lyell-Tayler with his mane of white hair and still as flamboyant as ever, and the short but handsome stature of Harold - being barely five feet tall - still using the Joachim bowing technique, when he said, "I noted that, as at Brighton, Ketèlbey's style of bowing differed from that of the rest, usually all the bows go the same way, but none of them agreed with Ketèlbey's". Harold remained with the Durban Civic Orchestra for some two years, becoming known as "Ket" by his fellow members of the orchestra and other musical associates, and it is said that whilst there his solo playing blossomed, and he was to be highly praised for several solo performances.

From here he moved with his family to Johannesburg where he was appointed leader and sub-conductor of the Johannesburg Municipal Orchestra, and where he again began teaching both violin and viola. Having established himself within his new role with the Johannesburg Orchestra, after a while he was given absence of leave when for some six months he took up the post of guest leader of the Cape Town Symphony Orchestra. For these six months he lived at the Cape Town home of Ralph Koorland, at that time acting leader of the same orchestra. In 1927 with his wife and two children Harold was to make a return trip to England, visiting his parents in Birmingham and brother Albert and wife Lottie in London, though neither Albert or indeed his parents were ever to make a trip to visit Harold at his home in South Africa.

In 1928 the Music Faculty of the University of Pretoria was formed - just thirty six miles away from Johannesburg, and for some years following its inception, Harold also took up the post of heading this Faculty, besides also now giving lessons in Pretoria once a week. By this time he was certainly a very busy man in the world of music, for besides his orchestral, solo and these other activities, he had by this time also formed his own "Ketèlbey String Quartet". With Harold on first violin, F.E. Pocock on second, Walter Swanson on viola and Eric Lefturch on cello, this quartet became one of the most successful in South Africa, and for several years gave concerts and performed regularly for the South African Broadcasting Corporation. When after a few years H. Lyell-Tayler had also left the Durban Civic Orchestra to move to Johannesburg, and become Musical Director of the South African

Broadcasting Corporation, this meant that the two old colleagues were to have regular contact again when Harold was to perform for the Broadcasting Corporation.

So it was that Harold worked out an excellent career in his sphere of music in South Africa, the last violin he owned being a cherished 'New Cremona'[26], and the success of this reserved and much liked and respected family man and professional musician was perhaps best epitomised when writing in March 1975 Harold Greenwood of Worcester, South Africa said of him:-

> "It was about 1929 that I first met Harold Ketèlbey - as a teacher, and I as a pupil of his in Pretoria, although I had attended some concerts given by his string quartet before making his acquaintance. At that time he lived in Johannesburg and came over once a week to Pretoria, where he had a few viola pupils as well as several violin pupils. He was a member of the Johannesburg Municipal Orchestra, being it's leader and sub-conductor.
>
> As a teacher he was remarkably patient, for some of his pupils, though willing, were slow to learn. For those of us who were "backward" he would demonstrate again and again how a tricky passage was to be played until we did it to his satisfaction. I never saw him lose his temper, but I fancy that he would have regarded that as not being an attitude of a good teacher.
>
> He was one of a small band of dedicated musicians who undertook the task of interesting the public of Johannesburg in music. The ultimate success of their efforts may be seen in the great variety of musical activities in that city today!"

In the process of time Harold was to gradually withdraw from the professional music scene and take up an interest in the business world. According to the Rev. Arnold Pierce-Jones - who maintained some contact with him - he showed much enterprise when he set up a business supplying requisites to the mining industry, and for the latter years of his life, after his wife Gertrude's death in 1954, he was to assist in the running of the family business Ketelbey & Gelletich (Pty.) Ltd., with his daughter and son. This successful mining business with two mines in Mica, North Eastern Transvaal,

---

26 Named after the home town of the famous Stradivarii family of string instrument makers.

and offices in Johannesburg had been previously set up under the auspices of his daughter Catherine and her husband, both geologists and who were mining pioneers of Pallabawa.

In a letter dated 18th July 1975 to William Neve, daughter Catherine Gelletich speaks of how dear her late father was to her, having died on the 17th April 1965 at the age of 82, and of her fond memories of him as an exceptionally fine violinist - playing many times Bach's *Chaconne* to the family, and listening spellbound to quartet rehearsals. She referred to her father as being a classicist with a great love of Chamber Music, and being a wonderful Bach player, and that although he realised that her uncle Albert's music was beloved by the public, he himself did not really appreciate it.

In the same letter she referred to it as being a great treat, when before the family moved out to South Africa, as a child she would occasionally visit her Uncle Albert in London, with her parents, when on each visit he would always present her with a beautiful present.

GENERAL INDEX COVERING PAGES 1 TO 138,
EXCLUDING KETÈLBEY'S COMPOSITIONS

INDEX OF KETÈLBEY'S COMPOSITONS REFERRED
TO COVERING PAGES 1 TO 138